Wh Intends for Us in His Commandments

WHAT WE CAN GAIN FROM GOD'S COMMANDMENTS

Lorenzo Hill

Scripture quotations taken from the Amplified® Bible (AMP),
Copyright © 2015 by The Lockman Foundation
Used by permission. www.Lockman.org

Scripture quotations taken from the Amplified® Bible (AMPC),
Copyright © 1954, 1958, 1962, 1964, 1965, 1987 by The Lockman Foundation
Used by permission. www.Lockman.org

Book Layout ©2017 BookDesignTemplates.com

What God Intends for Us in His Commandments / Lorenzo Hill. — 1st ed.
ISBN-13 978-0-9995992-1-1

Table of Contents

Dedicated To
Our Lord and Saviour
Jesus the Christ of Nazareth

GENESIS 2:8-9 KING JAMES VERSION (KJV)

[8] And the LORD God planted a garden eastward in Eden; and there he put the man whom he had formed.

[9] And out of the ground made the LORD God to grow every tree that is pleasant to the sight, and good for food; the tree of life also in the midst of the garden, and the tree of knowledge of good and evil.

DEUTERONOMY 28:9 KING JAMES VERSION (KJV)

[9] The Lord shall establish thee an holy people unto himself, as he hath sworn unto thee, if thou shalt keep the commandments of the Lord thy God, and walk in his ways.

ROMANS 2:13-16 KING JAMES VERSION (KJV)

[13] (For not the hearers of the law are just before God, but the doers of the law shall be justified.

[14] For when the Gentiles, which have not the law, do by nature the things contained in the law, these, having not the law, are a law unto themselves:

[15] Which shew the work of the law written in their hearts, their conscience also bearing witness, and their thoughts the mean while accusing or else excusing one another;)

[16] In the day when God shall judge the secrets of men by Jesus Christ according to my gospel.

CHAPTER 1

God Gave Commandments from the Beginning

Most people believe that men did not know about the commandments of God until God gave Israel the ten commandments. This is not the case. God has been providing the knowledge of what sin is from the very beginning. Not only are these included in scripture but they are found in many historical documents such as the code of Hammurabi. Those found outside of scripture have been corrupted though the influence of the tenets of God can be found in them. My mission is not to go into these but to identify that God has been actively providing commandments to men from the very beginning by using scripture. Here are a few examples from scripture.

- In the book of Genesis God spoke to all creation to be fruitful and multiply. He then gave further instruction to Adam that he could eat of any tree that bears fruit and that he could eat of all the green things which bear seeds but to not eat of the tree of the knowledge of good and evil. This shows that God understood that man could not handle this on his own so He placed this restriction on Adam. This to me shows God's desire for us is to remain innocent in our walk with Him.
- God made us and understands our limitations and our ability to make choices based on our use of our emotions (those outside of love) and misguided wants and desires and our ability to reason. He provided precepts to help us see when

these are out of the bounds of good (that they are harmful to us and others and outside the expression of love).

- He understands that even though we have these as a guide it does not mean we will choose to follow them. Here in the garden of Eden is the first example.

GENESIS 2:8-9 KING JAMES VERSION (KJV)[1]

[8] And the Lord God planted a garden eastward in Eden; and there he put the man whom he had formed.

[9] And out of the ground made the Lord God to grow every tree that is pleasant to the sight, and good for food; the tree of life also in the midst of the garden, and the tree of knowledge of good and evil.

GENESIS 2:15-17 KING JAMES VERSION (KJV)

[15] And the Lord God took the man, and put him into the garden of Eden to dress it and to keep it.

[16] And the Lord God commanded the man, saying, Of every tree of the garden thou mayest freely eat:

[17] But of the tree of the knowledge of good and evil, thou shalt not eat of it: for in the day that thou eatest thereof thou shalt surely die.

GENESIS 3:8-10 KING JAMES VERSION (KJV)

[8] And they heard the voice of the Lord God walking in the garden in the cool of the day: and Adam and his wife hid themselves from the presence of the Lord God amongst the trees of the garden.

[9] And the Lord God called unto Adam, and said unto him, Where art thou?

[10] And he said, I heard thy voice in the garden, and I was afraid, because I was naked; and I hid myself.

- Adam knew about marriage and the commitments required for it. In scripture Adam states that Eve was his wife. This was a concept not defined up to this point in printed words but the understanding and knowledge of it is shown in this verse below.

---

[1] All quotes from the King James and the Amplified bibles were taken from the site www.biblegateway.com. All King James Bible quotes are from an open source version. See copyright page for Amplified copyright permissions.

GENESIS 2:23-25 KING JAMES VERSION (KJV)
23 And Adam said, This is now bone of my bones, and flesh of my flesh: she shall be called Woman, because she was taken out of Man.
24 Therefore shall a man leave his father and his mother, and shall cleave unto his wife: and they shall be one flesh.
25 And they were both naked, the man and his wife, and were not ashamed.

- Scripture does not provide a blow by blow description of how things came about. Many times, only the results of man's choices and God's response are shown. Such is the case of the brothers Cain and Able. Cain and Able knew they were to offer a sacrifice to God. They both offered a sacrifice to God yet scripture does not provide any details on how they knew to do this. It is not until we get to the life of Moses in scripture do we find the guidelines from God in written form. In the scripture below, we are told of Cain and Able making an offering to God.

GENESIS 4:2-7 KING JAMES VERSION (KJV)
2 And she again bare his brother Abel. And Abel was a keeper of sheep, but Cain was a tiller of the ground.
3 And in process of time it came to pass, that Cain brought of the fruit of the ground an offering unto the Lord.
4 And Abel, he also brought of the firstlings of his flock and of the fat thereof. And the Lord had respect unto Abel and to his offering:
5 But unto Cain and to his offering he had not respect. And Cain was very wroth, and his countenance fell.
6 And the Lord said unto Cain, Why art thou wroth? and why is thy countenance fallen?
7 If thou doest well, shalt thou not be accepted? and if thou doest not well, sin lieth at the door. And unto thee shall be his desire, and thou shalt rule over him.
8 And Cain talked with Abel his brother: and it came to pass, when they were in the field, that Cain rose up against Abel his brother, and slew him.
9 And the Lord said unto Cain, Where is Abel thy brother? And he said, I know not: Am I my brother's keeper?
10 And he said, What hast thou done? the voice of thy brother's blood crieth unto me from the ground.

- Another example is Abraham. Abraham knew that it was wrong to lie about his wife being his sister to Abimilech the king of Gerar. The King also knew it was wrong to sleep with another man's wife. How did the knowledge of these choices arrive except somewhere along the line men were provided Godly instruction? In my studies I have come to the conclusion that the gospel was passed along verbally from person to person from the very beginning. It can be related to the fact of the length of time which many of them lived. If you get a biblical time line you can see how the time of their existence overlapped. In the beginning not much if any disease was present. I won't get into the fact that so many of them lived so long but I will point out that many scientists believe the body can last forever if there is not disease or trauma involved. Let's get back to scripture. Here is the account I mention here.

GENESIS 20:1-11 KING JAMES VERSION (KJV)

1 *And Abraham journeyed from thence toward the south country, and dwelled between Kadesh and Shur, and sojourned in Gerar.*

2 *And Abraham said of Sarah his wife, She is my sister: and Abimelech king of Gerar sent, and took Sarah.*

3 *But God came to Abimelech in a dream by night, and said to him, Behold, thou art but a dead man, for the woman which thou hast taken; for she is a man's wife.*

4 *But Abimelech had not come near her: and he said, Lord, wilt thou slay also a righteous nation?*

5 *Said he not unto me, She is my sister? and she, even she herself said, He is my brother: in the integrity of my heart and innocency of my hands have I done this.*

6 *And God said unto him in a dream, Yea, I know that thou didst this in the integrity of thy heart; for I also withheld thee from sinning against me: therefore suffered I thee not to touch her.*

7 *Now therefore restore the man his wife; for he is a prophet, and he shall pray for thee, and thou shalt live: and if thou restore her not, know thou that thou shalt surely die, thou, and all that are thine.*

8 *Therefore Abimelech rose early in the morning, and called all his servants, and told all these things in their ears: and the men were sore afraid.*

9 *Then Abimelech called Abraham, and said unto him, What hast thou done unto us? and what have I offended thee, that thou hast*

brought on me and on my kingdom a great sin? thou hast done deeds unto me that ought not to be done.
10 And Abimelech said unto Abraham, What sawest thou, that thou hast done this thing?
11 And Abraham said, Because I thought, Surely the fear of God is not in this place; and they will slay me for my wife's sake.

- Another account is provided with Joseph. Joseph knew that it was a sin to have sex with another man's wife. Again, no written commandments are mentioned about this prior to this point. Scripture demonstrates that Joseph knew about these but how? So, let's read a brief account of this act.

GENESIS 39:6-13 KING JAMES VERSION (KJV)
6 And he left all that he had in Joseph's hand; and he knew not ought he had, save the bread which he did eat. And Joseph was a goodly person, and well favoured.
7 And it came to pass after these things, that his master's wife cast her eyes upon Joseph; and she said, Lie with me.
8 But he refused, and said unto his master's wife, Behold, my master wotteth not what is with me in the house, and he hath committed all that he hath to my hand;
9 There is none greater in this house than I; neither hath he kept back any thing from me but thee, because thou art his wife: how then can I do this great wickedness, and sin against God?
10 And it came to pass, as she spake to Joseph day by day, that he hearkened not unto her, to lie by her, or to be with her.
11 And it came to pass about this time, that Joseph went into the house to do his business; and there was none of the men of the house there within.
12 And she caught him by his garment, saying, Lie with me: and he left his garment in her hand, and fled, and got him out.
13 And it came to pass, when she saw that he had left his garment in her hand, and was fled forth,

- One of the most prominent examples that the precepts of God were known long before written commandments were provided is that God is the only and true God. Abram or Abraham, as he was renamed by God, was from a land where there were many gods that were worshiped. How is it that Abram came to the understanding there is one true God? Let's us return to scripture.

GENESIS 17:1-3 KING JAMES VERSION (KJV)
¹ And when Abram was ninety years old and nine, the Lord appeared to Abram, and said unto him, I am the Almighty God; walk before me, and be thou perfect.
² And I will make my covenant between me and thee, and will multiply thee exceedingly.
³ And Abram fell on his face: and God talked with him, saying,

- Speaking again of Abraham how did he know to pay tithes to Melchizedek? This again is another example where a concept that is not published at this time is demonstrated. See this in the scripture which follows. Also note that Melchizedek is introduced as a priest of the Most-High God. I also am impressed that he served bread and wine to Abraham and blessed him. I pray that you can see the connection to Christ here. Maybe it is a stretch for you, but not me.

GENESIS 14:17-19 KING JAMES VERSION (KJV)
¹⁴ And when Abram heard that his brother was taken captive, he armed his trained servants, born in his own house, three hundred and eighteen, and pursued them unto Dan.
¹⁵ And he divided himself against them, he and his servants, by night, and smote them, and pursued them unto Hobah, which is on the left hand of Damascus.
¹⁶ And he brought back all the goods, and also brought again his brother Lot, and his goods, and the women also, and the people.
¹⁷ And the king of Sodom went out to meet him after his return from the slaughter of Chedorlaomer, and of the kings that were with him, at the valley of Shaveh, which is the king's dale.
¹⁸ And Melchizedek king of Salem brought forth bread and wine: and he was the priest of the most high God.
¹⁹ And he blessed him, and said, Blessed be Abram of the most high God, possessor of heaven and earth:
²⁰ And blessed be the most high God, which hath delivered thine enemies into thy hand. And he gave him tithes of all.
²¹ And the king of Sodom said unto Abram, Give me the persons, and take the goods to thyself.
²² And Abram said to the king of Sodom, I have lift up mine hand unto the Lord, the most high God, the possessor of heaven and earth,
²³ That I will not take from a thread even to a shoelatchet, and that I will not take any thing that is thine, lest thou shouldest say, I have made Abram rich:

²⁴ Save only that which the young men have eaten, and the portion of the men which went with me, Aner, Eshcol, and Mamre; let them take their portion.

Conclusion

God intended from the very beginning to keep man from harming himself and others but man has chosen to do what pleases himself and not God. God intends for us to be in a state of bliss which can only be obtained when we are free from the impact of evil in our lives. Many understand that they have the right to choose what they do with their lives. They don't understand that we were provided this ability to make this choice by the grace of God. This choice was implanted in us from the very beginning. As you can see God did not hinder Adam's ability to choose other than stating it would bring about death. Death in this sense carries two meanings. One is the temporal death or the separation of man's spirit from his body. The other is the spiritual death or the separation of man from the presence of God. God created us to commune with Him. We see this in the Garden of Eden and at Mount Horeb. It is detailed in many places in scripture. Is it unusual for God to communicate with us? Yes and No. Yes, for those whom God chooses. Take for instance Paul's experience on the road to Damascus. In scripture we see that Paul asked for the legal authority to persecute Christians. Yet God intervened. Here is that point in scripture.

ACTS 9:2-4 AMPLIFIED BIBLE (AMP)[2]
² and he asked for letters [of authority] from him to the synagogues at Damascus, so that if he found any men or women there belonging to [a]the Way [believers, followers of Jesus the Messiah], men and women alike, he could arrest them and bring them bound [with chains] to Jerusalem.
³ As he traveled he approached Damascus, and suddenly a light from heaven flashed around him [displaying the glory and majesty of Christ];
⁴ and he fell to the ground and heard a voice [from heaven] saying to him, "Saul, Saul, why are you persecuting and oppressing Me?"

---

[2] All quotes from the Amplified are provided under the Amplified Bible (AMP) Copyright © 2015 by The Lockman Foundation, La Habra, CA 90631. All rights reserved.

When it fits in with God's plan and there are those who are willing and God knows this will promote His work He speaks to men. God's communication with man started in the Garden and will continue until the end of time. Is it possible that God has been trying to communicate with you and you have chosen to ignore it? It is a sad state of affairs since in our day and time many preach that God stopped communicating with men with the death of the apostles. Don't believe it for it is not so. We even though we have been told about the spirit man has yet to accept this concept as real. I have experienced in my own life where my body and spirit were separated yet I wasn't dead. I guess God wanted me to have proof of this for this book to bring a blessing in your life.

It is a blessing to us that God has provided accounts in the scripture which detail how from the very beginning He has been looking into man's best interests. Though you may not think of it this way God's commandments are provided for man's best interest.

CHAPTER 2

What has Love got to Do with It?

We are told that God is love and that He created us so that we could share with Him in His creation. Evidence of this lies in the fact that God created us in His image. Is this act not one of love? Why would someone create something like himself unless He thinks very highly of His creation? Is there not more proof than in the fact that He provided for the well-being of His creation? He made a beautiful Garden for man's habitat.

GENESIS 1:26-31 KING JAMES VERSION (KJV)
26 And God said, Let us make man in our image, after our likeness: and let them have dominion over the fish of the sea, and over the fowl of the air, and over the cattle, and over all the earth, and over every creeping thing that creepeth upon the earth.
27 So God created man in his own image, in the image of God created he him; male and female created he them.
28 And God blessed them, and God said unto them, Be fruitful, and multiply, and replenish the earth, and subdue it: and have dominion over the fish of the sea, and over the fowl of the air, and over every living thing that moveth upon the earth.
29 And God said, Behold, I have given you every herb bearing seed, which is upon the face of all the earth, and every tree, in the which is the fruit of a tree yielding seed; to you it shall be for meat.
30 And to every beast of the earth, and to every fowl of the air, and to every thing that creepeth upon the earth, wherein there is life, I have given every green herb for meat: and it was so.
31 And God saw every thing that he had made, and, behold, it was very good. And the evening and the morning were the sixth day.

GENESIS 2:8-10 KING JAMES VERSION (KJV)
⁸ And the Lord God planted a garden eastward in Eden; and there he put the man whom he had formed.
⁹ And out of the ground made the Lord God to grow every tree that is pleasant to the sight, and good for food; the tree of life also in the midst of the garden, and the tree of knowledge of good and evil.
¹⁰ And a river went out of Eden to water the garden; and from thence it was parted, and became into four heads.

How about the fact that God wanted to provide for companionship for man? Does this not speak of how He loves us?

GENESIS 2:18-25 KING JAMES VERSION (KJV)
¹⁸ And the Lord God said, It is not good that the man should be alone; I will make him an help meet for him.
¹⁹ And out of the ground the Lord God formed every beast of the field, and every fowl of the air; and brought them unto Adam to see what he would call them: and whatsoever Adam called every living creature, that was the name thereof.
²⁰ And Adam gave names to all cattle, and to the fowl of the air, and to every beast of the field; but for Adam there was not found an help meet for him.
²¹ And the Lord God caused a deep sleep to fall upon Adam, and he slept: and he took one of his ribs, and closed up the flesh instead thereof;
²² And the rib, which the Lord God had taken from man, made he a woman, and brought her unto the man.
²³ And Adam said, This is now bone of my bones, and flesh of my flesh: she shall be called Woman, because she was taken out of Man.
²⁴ Therefore shall a man leave his father and his mother, and shall cleave unto his wife: and they shall be one flesh.
²⁵ And they were both naked, the man and his wife, and were not ashamed.

GENESIS 2:18-25 AMPLIFIED BIBLE (AMP)
¹⁸ Now the Lord God said, "It is not good (beneficial) for the man to be alone; I will make him a helper [one who balances him—a counterpart who is] [a]suitable and complementary for him."
¹⁹ So the Lord God formed out of the ground every animal of the field and every bird of the air, and brought them to Adam to see what he would call them; and whatever the man called a living creature, that was its name. ²⁰ And the man gave names to all the livestock, and to the birds of the air, and to every animal of the

field; but for Adam there was not found a helper [that was] suitable (a companion) for him.
²¹ So the Lord God caused a deep sleep to fall upon Adam; and while he slept, He took one of his ribs and closed up the flesh at that place.
²² And the rib which the Lord God had taken from the man He made (fashioned, formed) into a woman, and He brought her and presented her to the man.
²³ Then Adam said,
"This is now bone of my bones,
And flesh of my flesh;
She shall be called Woman,
Because she was taken out of Man."
²⁴ For this reason a man shall leave his father and his mother, and shall be joined to his wife; and they shall become one flesh.
²⁵ And the man and his wife were both naked and were not ashamed or embarrassed.

FOOTNOTES:
Genesis 2:18 Lit like his opposite.

How about the fact that God has not only seen to our physical needs? Has He not provided the air we breathe and the water we drink and a body built for life? He also has provided for our spiritual welfare. So, He began teaching us by providing instruction (commandments). The first commandment was to be fruitful and multiply. Then He provided guidance to help prevent us from making choices that would provide ongoing damage. First was the commandment to not eat (take into our being) of the tree of the knowledge of good and evil.

GENESIS 2:15-17 KING JAMES VERSION (KJV)
¹⁵ And the Lord God took the man, and put him into the garden of Eden to dress it and to keep it.
¹⁶ And the Lord God commanded the man, saying, Of every tree of the garden thou mayest freely eat:
¹⁷ But of the tree of the knowledge of good and evil, thou shalt not eat of it: for in the day that thou eatest thereof thou shalt surely die.

Is this not love that a parent will provide good directions for his children to prevent them from making the wrong choices? Oh, did I fail to mention it is love that that is demonstrated in the fact that God allowed man to have the freedom to be able to choose to follow or not follow His direction (commandments)? Is this love or not? Do you not correct your own children to keep them from harming themselves when danger is present? Do you not teach them to be careful with knives so they won't cut themselves or to take care around fire to keep from being burned or to not put things in their mouths that can harm them? Scripture goes on and on with God's guidance which He has provided for man. Which for me leads to the Ten Commandments. We'll discuss more about these later in another chapter.

Throughout the scripture we are told about the love of God. How about the ones below.

JOHN 3:16-21 KING JAMES VERSION (KJV)
16 For God so loved the world, that he gave his only begotten Son, that whosoever believeth in him should not perish, but have everlasting life.

17 For God sent not his Son into the world to condemn the world; but that the world through him might be saved.

18 He that believeth on him is not condemned: but he that believeth not is condemned already, because he hath not believed in the name of the only begotten Son of God.

19 And this is the condemnation, that light is come into the world, and men loved darkness rather than light, because their deeds were evil.

20 For every one that doeth evil hateth the light, neither cometh to the light, lest his deeds should be reproved.

21 But he that doeth truth cometh to the light, that his deeds may be made manifest, that they are wrought in God.

EPHESIANS 2:3-5 KING JAMES VERSION (KJV)
3 Among whom also we all had our conversation in times past in the lusts of our flesh, fulfilling the desires of the flesh and of the mind; and were by nature the children of wrath, even as others.

4 But God, who is rich in mercy, for his great love wherewith he loved us,

5 Even when we were dead in sins, hath quickened us together with Christ, (by grace ye are saved;)

Note the word grace. It is how we can perceive the love of God that He chooses to look for our wellbeing even though it is undeserved or unmerited. He has provided for our release from the penalty of sin just by our choice to allow Jesus of Nazareth to be the one punished for what we have done. He prepared a way out for us even though we don't deserve it. Read the following scripture.

> ***ROMANS 8:38-39 KING JAMES VERSION (KJV)***
> ***38** For I am persuaded, that neither death, nor life, nor angels, nor principalities, nor powers, nor things present, nor things to come,*
> ***39** Nor height, nor depth, nor any other creature, shall be able to separate us from the love of God, which is in Christ Jesus our Lord.*
> ***MICAH 6:7-9 KING JAMES VERSION (KJV)***
> ***7** Will the Lord be pleased with thousands of rams, or with ten thousands of rivers of oil? shall I give my firstborn for my transgression, the fruit of my body for the sin of my soul?*
> ***8** He hath shewed thee, O man, what is good; and what doth the Lord require of thee, but to do justly, and to love mercy, and to walk humbly with thy God?*
> ***9** The Lord's voice crieth unto the city, and the man of wisdom shall see thy name: hear ye the rod, and who hath appointed it.*

As can be seen in the scripture above God's love is beyond reproach and has no limits. I can continue to point out more and more how the scripture details the fact that God loves us. I believe you should be able to get the point. God because of His love for us takes on the responsibility for seeing that correction for sin is on Him. He only requires us to accept His offer.

God has always tried to protect us from ourselves but out of love He allows us to choose to do as we wish. He only holds us accountable for our choices when we are able to intelligently discern that we are making wrong choices. All Little children, even though they can do acts which are considered sinful, are covered by the blood of Christ until they reach the age at which they are able to intelligently comprehend the fact that the choices they are making are either good or evil. Sin can only be committed when an intelligent decision is made to go against the tenets of God (which everyone has embedded in his conscience). This is a difficult concept for us to see in most cases. The fact that children cannot sin is not well defined in scripture. Have you not heard how there are children who have a lack of compassion or feelings of remorse for their actions? Consider the fact that children will intentionally hurt you or others or that they will test the waters to see what they can get away with. Have you not ever held a baby who will strike at you in anger when they are hurt? These are mechanisms built into them by design. Do we not have to correct our children to keep them in line? Yes, children can learn to sin and uncorrected they will usually choose to remain in these patterns.

There are also those who because of their medical conditions are unable to have the ability to know to choose between good and evil. I believe they too are under the protection of Christ Jesus' sacrifice for our sins. This again points to His love. The bible only hints at this precept but it is more plainly explained by the following scripture.

MORONI 8:5-18 THE BOOK OF MORMON

5 For if I have learned the truth, there have been disputations among you concerning the baptism of your little children.

6 And now my son, I desire that ye should labor diligently, that this gross error should be removed from among you; for, for this intent I have written this epistle.

7 For immediately after I had learned these things of you, I inquired of the Lord concerning the matter.

8 And the word of the Lord came to me by the power of the Holy Ghost, saying, Listen to the words of Christ, your Redeemer, your Lord, and your God.

9 Behold, I came into the world not to call the righteous, but sinners to repentance; the whole need no physician, but they that are sick; wherefore little children are whole, for they are not capable of committing sin; wherefore the curse of Adam is taken from them in me, that it hath no

power over them; and the law of circumcision is done away in me.

10 And after this manner did the Holy Ghost manifest the word of God unto me; wherefore my beloved son, I know that it is solemn mockery before God, that ye should baptize little children.

11 Behold I say unto you, that this thing shall ye teach, repentance and baptism unto those who are accountable and capable of committing sin; yea, teach parents that they must repent and be baptized, and humble themselves as their little children, and they shall all be saved with their

little children: and their little children need no repentance, neither baptism.

12 Behold, baptism is unto repentance to the fulfilling the commandments unto the remission of sins.

13 But little children are alive in Christ, even from the foundation of the world; if not so, God is a partial God, and also a changeable God, and a respecter to persons; for how many little children have died without baptism.

14 Wherefore, if little children could not be saved without baptism, these must have gone to an endless hell.

15 Behold I say unto you, that he that supposeth that little children need baptism, is in the gall of bitterness, and in the bonds of iniquity; for he hath neither faith, hope, nor charity; wherefore, should he be cut off while in the thought, he must go down to hell.
16 For awful is the wickedness to suppose that God saveth one child because of baptism, and the other must perish because he hath no baptism.
17 Wo be unto him that shall pervert the ways of the Lord after this manner, for they shall perish, except they repent.
18 Behold, I speak with boldness, having authority from God; and I fear not what man can do; for perfect love casteth out all fear; and I am filled with charity, which is everlasting love; wherefore all children are alike unto me; wherefore I love little children with a perfect love; and they are all alike, and partakers of salvation.
ROMANS 2:14-16 KING JAMES VERSION (KJV)
14 For when the Gentiles, which have not the law, do by nature the things contained in the law, these, having not the law, are a law unto themselves:
15 Which shew the work of the law written in their hearts, their conscience also bearing witness, and their thoughts the mean while accusing or else excusing one another;)
16 In the day when God shall judge the secrets of men by Jesus Christ according to my gospel.

The above scriptures show how God has made provision for those who have not had the opportunity to hear the gospel and accept Jesus in this life. Is this not an example of how far the love of God is extended?

Then comes one of the most difficult of all things to understand about the love of God. It is why and how He allows the innocent to suffer at the hand of evil doers. This has been a concept that has puzzled man since Cain slew his brother Able. Many have written books which try to examine why bad things happen to good people. There has even been a very popular book written with this title which explores this concept. I have read and still have a copy in my library.

We hear about murder, robbery, rape and much more going on in this world all the time. Scripture details the brutality which man treats his fellow man in gory detail. So how is the love of God displayed in these instances? What I am led to point out is as follows:

1. We are told in scripture that God will punish those who commit these acts.

2. We are told that none of us are truly innocent and that we all deserve to be punished for our sin.
3. We are told in scripture that God does not delight in the suffering of the innocent.
4. We are told God will comfort those who morn and who have been treated unjustly.
5. No one is exempt from the pangs of evil deeds. This is harsh, yet sin is harsh, and unless its harshness is revealed none will abhor it.
6. Lastly there is the source of all evil; that evil one Satan, or the Devil or however you like to term him. Scripture tells us we battle not against flesh and blood but spiritual wickedness in high places.
7. We all want to say that God should be the one who should protect us from being wronged but don't want to take any credit for our role in the acts of sin and its attributes. It is a harsh reality that we just don't want to consider.
8. It is easy to question why does God allow evil to happen to good people, but Jesus says there is none good except God. Scripture also states that God has to allow evil so that the evil can be punished for crimes committed and that we can see the issues that evil brings with it. He will provide consolation to the innocent in Heaven.
9. Evil acts and its suffering will only be done away with when we all turn to God after the return of Christ Jesus.
10. And shall we not consider those who suffer natural disasters? That God does not consider those people any worse sinners than anyone else.
11. Most of us will not get the true meaning of this until we are in the presence of the Father. So, until then, the question "why" will remain with most of us.
12. Just as Job questioned why he had to suffer we too have to suffer through evil in this world.

In the scripture below we are given an explanation of why bad things happen to good people. God has to allow evil to be performed so that He can justly judge that evil has been performed. Therefore, without the fulfillment of evil acts He cannot punish those who perform it. Even the law today only punishes those who have committed a crime. Often, we know a crime is in a person's heart but until they complete the act the law can do nothing. Case in point, when a restraining order is issued, the law cannot imprison a person until he breaks the provisions of the order. We have seen time and time again where the person violates the order doing harm to the innocent party. We then can enact the penalty but the innocent suffers as a result. God states that He will recompense the innocent in heaven. This is a difficult thing to take but maybe we will understand it fully someday. We also need to see evil for what it is and the results it brings so that we can learn the lesson that we should abstain from it.

GENESIS 6:4-6 KING JAMES VERSION (KJV)

⁴ There were giants in the earth in those days; and also after that, when the sons of God came in unto the daughters of men, and they bare children to them, the same became mighty men which were of old, men of renown.

⁵ And God saw that the wickedness of man was great in the earth, and that every imagination of the thoughts of his heart was only evil continually.

⁶ And it repented the Lord that he had made man on the earth, and it grieved him at his heart.

GENESIS 6:4-6 AMPLIFIED BIBLE (AMP)

⁴ There were Nephilim (men of stature, notorious men) on the earth in those days—and also afterward—when the sons of God lived with the daughters of men, and they gave birth to their children. These were the mighty men who were of old, men of renown (great reputation, fame).

⁵ The Lord saw that the wickedness (depravity) of man was great on the earth, and that every imagination or intent of the thoughts of his heart were only evil continually.

⁶ The Lord [a]regretted that He had made mankind on the earth, and He was [deeply] grieved in His heart.

FOOTNOTES:

Genesis 6:6 The expressions of regret and grief seen here do not mean that God acknowledged the creation of man as a mistake on His part. God is omniscient, knowing all things (Ps 139:16) and He knew that mankind would come into sin and wickedness. God grieved over the sin of man because it was appropriate for Him to do so.

PSALM 14:1-3 KING JAMES VERSION (KJV)

¹ The fool hath said in his heart, There is no God. They are corrupt, they have done abominable works, there is none that doeth good.

2 The Lord looked down from heaven upon the children of men, to see if there were any that did understand, and seek God.

3 They are all gone aside, they are all together become filthy: there is none that doeth good, no, not one.

EPHESIANS 6:11-13 KING JAMES VERSION (KJV)

11 Put on the whole armour of God, that ye may be able to stand against the wiles of the devil.

12 For we wrestle not against flesh and blood, but against principalities, against powers, against the rulers of the darkness of this world, against spiritual wickedness in high places.

13 Wherefore take unto you the whole armour of God, that ye may be able to withstand in the evil day, and having done all, to stand.

ALMA 10:48-54 THE BOOK OF MORMON

48 And when Amulek saw the pains of the women and children who were consuming in the fire,he was also pained; and he said unto Alma, How can we witness this awful scene? 49 Therefore let us stretch forth our hands, and exercise the power of God which is in us, and save them from the flames.

50 But Alma said unto him, The Spirit constraineth me that I must not stretch forth mine hand; for behold, the Lord receiveth them up unto himself, in glory;

51 And he doth suffer that they may do this thing, or that the people may do this thing unto them, according to the hardness of their hearts, that the judgments which he shall exercise upon them in his wrath, may be just; 52 And the blood of the innocent shall stand as a witness against them, yea, and cry mightily against them at the last day.

53 Now Amulek said unto Alma, Behold, perhaps they will burn us also.

54 And Alma said, Be it according to the will of the Lord. But behold, our work is not finished; therefore they burn us not.

ACTS 10:33-35 KING JAMES VERSION (KJV)

33 Immediately therefore I sent to thee; and thou hast well done that thou art come. Now therefore are we all here present before God, to hear all things that are commanded thee of God.

34 Then Peter opened his mouth, and said, Of a truth I perceive that God is no respecter of persons:

35 But in every nation he that feareth him, and worketh righteousness, is accepted with him.

> ***LUKE 13:1-5 KING JAMES VERSION (KJV)***
> *¹ There were present at that season some that told him of the Galilaeans, whose blood Pilate had mingled with their sacrifices.*
> *² And Jesus answering said unto them, Suppose ye that these Galilaeans were sinners above all the Galilaeans, because they suffered such things?*
> *³ I tell you, Nay: but, except ye repent, ye shall all likewise perish.*
> *⁴ Or those eighteen, upon whom the tower in Siloam fell, and slew them, think ye that they were sinners above all men that dwelt in Jerusalem?*
> *⁵ I tell you, Nay: but, except ye repent, ye shall all likewise perish.*

I will share an experience in my own life. At the age of 14 months my youngest daughter was severely burned. In the hours up to the time when she was miraculously healed, I was in intense turmoil and anguish. I could not bear to see her suffer. My pain was mental but hers was both physical and mental. I questioned whether she was being punished because of my past sins or those of someone in my family? I did not ever come up with an answer even after her healing. All I knew was that the suffering was over and I had to praise God for it. Yet, on the other side is my cousin who has had to suffer most of her life as a result a childhood accident in which most of her upper body, including her face, was badly burned and scarred. Look at the years of anguish and suffering she has had to endure yet she continued on in life living it as best she could. Both were innocent. I can't explain why one was healed and the other one was not. By our reasoning neither one of them deserved the suffering caused by these accidents.

Where is God's love in all of this? All I am led to share is that we are allowed to continue to sin until the end comes just as those before the flood. Refer to the scripture above Genesis 6:4-6. God does allow these things to happen and we will not gain insight for all of this until we are at His feet. Even though I now know God wants us to see evil for what it is and that we are all subject to it just as Job was, it is not always consoling nor will we always understand. Jesus told his disciples in this world you will have trouble and how true that is.

> ***JOHN 16:33 KING JAMES VERSION (KJV)***
> *³³ These things I have spoken unto you, that in me ye might have peace. In the world ye shall have tribulation: but be of good cheer; I have overcome the world.*

Look at how God approaches Job who challenged God about his righteousness and undeserved suffering.

JOB 40:1-24 AMPLIFIED BIBLE (AMP)

Job: What Can I Say?
1 Then the Lord said to Job,
2 "Will the faultfinder contend with the Almighty? Let him who disputes with God answer it."
3 Then Job replied to the Lord and said,
4 "Behold, I am of little importance and contemptible; what can I reply to You? I lay my hand on my mouth.
5 "I have spoken once, but I will not reply again—Indeed, twice [I have answered], and I will add nothing further." God Questions Job
6 Then the Lord answered Job out of the whirlwind, saying,
7 "Now [a]gird up your loins (prepare yourself) like a man, And I will ask you, and you instruct Me.
8 "Will you really annul My judgment and set it aside as void? Will you condemn Me [your God] that you may [appear to] be righteous and justified?
9 "Have you an arm like God, And can you thunder with a voice like His?
10 "Adorn yourself with eminence and dignity [since you question the Almighty], And array yourself with honor and majesty.
11 "Pour out the overflowings of your wrath, And look at everyone who is proud and make him low.
12 Look at everyone who is proud, and humble him, And [if you are so able] tread down the wicked where they stand.
13 "[Crush and] hide them in the dust together; Shut them up in the hidden place [the house of death].
14 "[If you can do all this, Job, proving your divine power] then I [God] will also praise you and acknowledge That your own right hand can save you. God's Power Shown in Creatures
15 "Behold now, [b]Behemoth, which I created as well as you; He eats grass like an ox.
16 "See now, his strength is in his loins And his power is in the muscles and sinews of his belly.
17 "He sways his tail like a cedar; The tendons of his thighs are twisted and knit together [like a rope].
18 "His bones are tubes of bronze; His [c]limbs are like bars of iron.
19 "He is the first [in magnitude and power] of the works of God; [Only] He who made him can bring near His sword [to master him].
20 "Surely the mountains bring him food, And all the wild animals play there.

²¹ "He lies down under the lotus plants, In the hidden shelter of the reeds in the marsh.
²² "The lotus plants cover him with their shade; The willows of the brook surround him.
²³ "If a river rages and overflows, he does not tremble; He is confident, though the Jordan [River] swells and rushes against his mouth.
²⁴ "Can anyone capture him when he is on watch,
Or pierce his nose with barbs [to trap him]?
FOOTNOTES:
Job 40:7 See note 38:3.
Job 40:15 Or the hippopotamus. Although Behemoth cannot be identified with certainty, the biblical description seems most like the hippopotamus. In ancient times it may have been even more formidable than today. In Job's day the hippopotamus was the largest known creature, was commonly found in the lower Nile River, and may also have existed in the Jordan.
Job 40:18 Lit bones.

JOB 42:1-6 AMPLIFIED BIBLE (AMP)
Job's Confession
¹ Then Job answered the Lord and said,
² "I know that You can do all things, And that no thought or purpose of Yours can be restrained.
³ "[You said to me] 'Who is this that darkens and obscures counsel [by words] without knowledge?' Therefore [I now see] I have [rashly] uttered that which I did not understand, Things too wonderful for me, which I did not know.
⁴ 'Hear, please, and I will speak; I will ask You, and You instruct [and answer] me.'
⁵ "I had heard of You [only] by the hearing of the ear, But now my [spiritual] eye sees You.
⁶ "Therefore I retract [my words and hate myself] And I repent in dust and ashes."

Conclusion

God has defined love for us in the scripture. It is this:
1 CORINTHIANS 13:1-13 AMPLIFIED BIBLE (AMP)
The Excellence of Love
¹ If I speak with the tongues of men and of angels, but have not [a]love [for others growing out of God's love for me], then I have

become only a noisy gong or a clanging cymbal [just an annoying distraction].

² And if I have the gift of prophecy [and speak a new message from God to the people], and understand all mysteries, and [possess] all knowledge; and if I have all [sufficient] faith so that I can remove mountains, but do not have love [reaching out to others], I am nothing.

³ If I give all my possessions to feed the poor, and if I surrender my body [b]to be burned, but do not have love, it does me no good at all.

⁴ Love endures with patience and serenity, love is kind and thoughtful, and is not jealous or envious; love does not brag and is not proud or arrogant. ⁵ It is not rude; it is not self-seeking, it is not provoked [nor overly sensitive and easily angered]; it does not take into account a wrong endured.

⁶ It does not rejoice at injustice, but rejoices with the truth [when right and truth prevail].

⁷ Love bears all things [regardless of what comes], believes all things [looking for the best in each one], hopes all things [remaining steadfast during difficult times], endures all things [without weakening].

⁸ Love never fails [it never fades nor ends]. But as for prophecies, they will pass away; as for tongues, they will cease; as for the gift of special knowledge, it will pass away.

⁹ For we know in part, and we prophesy in part [for our knowledge is fragmentary and incomplete].

¹⁰ But when that which is complete and perfect comes, that which is incomplete and partial will pass away.

¹¹ When I was a child, I talked like a child, I thought like a child, I reasoned like a child; when I became a man, I did away with childish things.

¹² For now [in this time of imperfection] we see in a mirror dimly [a blurred reflection, a riddle, an enigma], but then [when the time of perfection comes we will see reality] face to face. Now I know in part [just in fragments], but then I will know fully, just as I have been fully known [by God].

¹³ And now there remain: faith [abiding trust in God and His promises], hope [confident expectation of eternal salvation], love [unselfish love for others growing out of God's love for me], these three [the choicest graces]; but the greatest of these is love.

FOOTNOTES:

1 Corinthians 13:1 I.e. a profound thoughtfulness and unselfish concern for other believers regardless of their circumstances or station in life.

1 Corinthians 13:3 Early mss read so that I may boast, i.e. as a martyr.

As we can see from the above scripture love is a complex emotion which carries with it actions which are not self-centered. Love is more than an expression. It carries with it actions which are clearly definable. They are actions which work to provide for the good of others first and sacrificing our own needs so that we share in happiness and all that we have. It should also be pointed out that the scripture above is about choosing to do what we can to provide for the good of others which in turn is a benefit for all. Therefore, I can choose to be kind because I love. I can choose to be patient because I love. I can choose to not be jealous because I love. As you examine each of these verses you can gain understanding that love is the basis of each of these actions or attributes.

There are imitations but the true essence of each of these actions is love. Without love none of the above actions have any meaning. They are empty expressions performed out of pretense and are not genuine.

All of these are expressed in the way God reacts toward us. Even to the point of sacrificing His Son Jesus the Christ of Nazareth for our sins.

JOHN 15:12-14 AMPLIFIED BIBLE (AMP)

Disciples' Relation to Each Other

[12] "This is My commandment, that you [a]love and unselfishly seek the best for one another, just as I have loved you.

[13] No one has greater love [nor stronger commitment] than to lay down his own life for his friends.

[14] You are my friends if you keep on doing what I command you.

Jesus' answer to man is man is capable of fulfilling all commandments by following His statement on love. Let's start with this in the Old Testament:

DEUTERONOMY 10:12-13 KING JAMES VERSION (KJV)

[12] And now, Israel, what doth the Lord thy God require of thee, but to fear the Lord thy God, to walk in all his ways, and to love him, and to serve the Lord thy God with all thy heart and with all thy soul,

*13 To keep the commandments of the Lord, and his statutes, which
I command thee this day for thy good?*
DEUTERONOMY 30:6 KING JAMES VERSION (KJV)
*6 And the Lord thy God will circumcise thine heart, and the heart of
thy seed, to love the Lord thy God with all thine heart, and with all
thy soul, that thou mayest live.*

Now as Jesus restated this in the New Testament.
MATTHEW 22:36-40 KING JAMES VERSION (KJV)
36 Master, which is the great commandment in the law?
*37 Jesus said unto him, Thou shalt love the Lord thy God with all thy
heart, and with all thy soul, and with all thy mind.*
38 This is the first and great commandment.
*39 And the second is like unto it, Thou shalt love thy neighbour as
thyself.*
40 On these two commandments hang all the law and the prophets.

As can be seen from the above scriptures, all that God does and
says for man are out of His love and His expectation is no less for man.
He wants man to treat Him and his fellow brothers and sisters with the
same love. Finally, God does not show favoritism. Not only does He
love us but He treats each of us equally. He treats us all in accordance
with His Divine justice and mercy as scripture states God is no
respecter of persons and we all share in His loving providence.
MATTHEW 5:44-46 KING JAMES VERSION (KJV)
*44 But I say unto you, Love your enemies, bless them that curse you,
do good to them that hate you, and pray for them which
despitefully use you, and persecute you;*
*45 That ye may be the children of your Father which is in heaven: for
he maketh his sun to rise on the evil and on the good, and sendeth
rain on the just and on the unjust.*
*46 For if ye love them which love you, what reward have ye? do not
even the publicans the same?*
ACTS 10:33-35 KING JAMES VERSION (KJV)
*33 Immediately therefore I sent to thee; and thou hast well done
that thou art come. Now therefore are we all here present before
God, to hear all things that are commanded thee of God.*
*34 Then Peter opened his mouth, and said, Of a truth I perceive that
God is no respecter of persons:*
*35 But in every nation he that feareth him, and worketh
righteousness, is accepted with him.*

Note Jesus' statement in Matthew 5:45 that is God does good for
all of us; the good, the bad and the evil. We all share in His goodness

alike. God does not send evil, He only restrains it or allows it to be unleashed for us to learn the effects of sin. He gives love for the sake of the benefits it can provide looking for nothing else. He expects the same from us. Through His love we have the gift of life and all the benefits and pitfalls that come with it.

CHAPTER 3

Rewards and Punishment

It would not be fitting to discuss commandments without discussing the benefits and issues which face us when we don't follow the commandments. First consider what justice is and why God is the one who defines it. Consider the conversation between God and Job.

JOB 8:2-4 KING JAMES VERSION (KJV)
² How long wilt thou speak these things? and how long shall the words of thy mouth be like a strong wind?
³ Doth God pervert judgment? or doth the Almighty pervert justice?
⁴ If thy children have sinned against him, and he have cast them away for their transgression;

ISAIAH 58:1-3 KING JAMES VERSION (KJV)
¹ Cry aloud, spare not, lift up thy voice like a trumpet, and shew my people their transgression, and the house of Jacob their sins.
² Yet they seek me daily, and delight to know my ways, as a nation that did righteousness, and forsook not the ordinance of their God: they ask of me the ordinances of justice; they take delight in approaching to God.
³ Wherefore have we fasted, say they, and thou seest not? wherefore have we afflicted our soul, and thou takest no knowledge? Behold, in the day of your fast ye find pleasure, and exact all your labours.

God is the one who made us in His image. He fully understands the limits and bounds wherein we can function best. Have you ever seen the show "Father Knows Best" and how he always was able to get it right when it came to solving family problems? Or the wisdom that Beaver's dad displayed when it came to dealing with all the situations

27

Beaver always got into on "Leave It to Beaver?" Have you considered that God is like that? That when it comes to solving family issues He knows best. Should not the maker know the limitations of His creation? Most of the time, whenever we make a decision, we don't have a clue about all that we create or what the results of our decisions will be. We don't have the knowledge to fully evaluate what we are putting into motion. Life to us is like a maze. We can only see as far as the next corner and maybe not that far. So, like Beaver, don't we need the wisdom of a wise Father to not only rescue us from our misguided choices but to guide us before we make a mess or to help us clean up the messes we have made? The Lord is helping me to understand that the commandments are the wisdom of a loving, wise Father providing insights in how to make it through the maze of life and to help us understand that we can't do it without Him. Does scripture not tell us within each portion of His creation there is a set of laws or rules which governs that portion of His creation? Hasn't science proven that, if we are diligent, we can discover the laws which govern the world around us. Is man any different that he should not also be considered in the same light as the rest of God's creation? Of course, I should point out that man is a little different since he was created with the ability to choose whether to follow in the design for him. Of course, scripture also tells us that choice was also provided to the angels in heaven as well. This is how Satan came about and his demons. They choose not to follow God's design for them. More on this later.

Consider the description we are provided in how God created the universe. We are first provided with the account of the spiritual creation. Here we are shown God's wisdom at work. He is shown in the process of using His wise consideration of how things would fit together prior to the actual implementation or when creation took its final form. See the book of Genesis chapters 1-2. I will not duplicate it all here but consider the following:

GENESIS 2:1-6 KING JAMES VERSION (KJV)
¹ Thus the heavens and the earth were finished, and all the host of them.
² And on the seventh day God ended his work which he had made; and he rested on the seventh day from all his work which he had made.
³ And God blessed the seventh day, and sanctified it: because that in it he had rested from all his work which God created and made.

⁴ These are the generations of the heavens and of the earth when they were created, in the day that the Lord God made the earth and the heavens,
⁵ And every plant of the field before it was in the earth, and every herb of the field before it grew: for the Lord God had not caused it to rain upon the earth, and there was not a man to till the ground.
⁶ But there went up a mist from the earth, and watered the whole face of the ground.

See the progression described here. Seeds were in the ground but plants had yet to appear and how the ground had to be watered prior to plants appearing. Is this not the description of His wisdom at work?

Because of my training as a chemical engineer, I can appreciate this. It's like when we make the calculations to produce a process to come up with an end product. We understand that the equations don't tell the whole story. They are only our way of expressing what we understand about the way the creation works and they do not always work in actuality the way we have observed. Therefore, we make a sample of the procedure (mock up) to test it out. We call this a pilot plant. Then after we figure out what works and what doesn't (where the bugs are) we build the actual plant to put the process into production. Even after we have gone through the process of careful planning many times the full-scale production model many times does not work as anticipated and we again have to make some tweaks to achieve the desired result. Isn't it wonderful that God knows all the parameters where with we are created so in His infinite wisdom, He will not fail to achieve His final goal?

I can see all this in the way God went about making the universe. Yes, I can see His intelligence and careful planning being used in the creation. I know there are many who try to explain this away but I can see the intelligence in the creation, not chaos or just random events taking place with no design or purpose. The Holy Spirit has helped me to see beyond the words on the page. So, when I look at God's work in Genesis, I can see how He carefully and purposefully made the creation and how each part compliments the whole. Take for example our solar system. Each segment fitting together in a definable pattern. Through our observation of the planets we can depict the movement of each of the planets around the sun. We have come up with calculations which can depict the way the planets influence each other. This is not just a modern invention. We have discovered even in antiquity that men have been able to depict the movement and interactions of the planets. We have figured out that each portion impacts the other and that without that interaction things will go all wrong. How is this possible without some intelligent intent being involved? Take a careful look into the creation account. Here in the description provided in Genesis we can see how carefully and thoughtfully God made the creation. It was not just a group of random actions but a careful plan being considered before being placed into the actual construction of each portion.

GENESIS 1:13-15 KING JAMES VERSION (KJV)

13 And the evening and the morning were the third day.

14 And God said, Let there be lights in the firmament of the heaven to divide the day from the night; and let them be for signs, and for seasons, and for days, and years:

15 And let them be for lights in the firmament of the heaven to give light upon the earth: and it was so.

GENESIS 1:13-15 AMPLIFIED BIBLE (AMP)

13 And there was evening and there was morning, a third day.

14 Then God said, "Let there be light-bearers (sun, moon, stars) in the expanse of the heavens to separate the day from the night, and let them be useful for signs (tokens) [of God's provident care], and for marking seasons, days, and years;

15 and let them be useful as lights in the expanse of the heavens to provide light on the earth"; and it was so, [just as He commanded].

PSALM 8:2-4 KING JAMES VERSION (KJV)

2 Out of the mouth of babes and sucklings hast thou ordained strength because of thine enemies, that thou mightest still the enemy and the avenger.

3 When I consider thy heavens, the work of thy fingers, the moon and the stars, which thou hast ordained;

4 What is man, that thou art mindful of him? and the son of man, that thou visitest him?

JEREMIAH 31:34-36 AMPLIFIED BIBLE (AMP)

34 And each man will no longer teach his neighbor and his brother, saying, 'Know the Lord,' for they will all know Me [through personal experience], from the least of them to the greatest," says the Lord. "For I will forgive their wickedness, and I will no longer remember their sin."

35 Thus says the Lord, Who gives the sun for light by day And the fixed order of the moon and of the stars for light by night, Who stirs

up the sea's roaring billows or stills the waves when they roar; The
Lord of hosts is His name:
36 "If this fixed order departs From before Me," says the Lord, "Then
the descendants of Israel also will cease From being a nation before
Me forever."

The Holy Spirit can help you see between the lines in the scripture how God carefully considered how each item would fit together and how each segment would depend on the others. How He carefully planned each step so that each part would come out just right without error and without failure. How He made sure each segment would meet His original intent for all of it. He used a careful stepwise plan in the creation. Each part independently designed yet all dependent on the other part with proper influence and cooperation. Each portion of His creation is a testament of His ability, creativity power and love. You see God set in motion laws that the planets abide. That is how we can determine their movement and times and dates for these.

I can imagine the joy He experienced when He completed each portion and said "it is good." I have experienced similar reactions when I design a pipeline and it is completed. I make the calculations to determine what needs to go into the design. I have to decide based on the calculations how large the pipe has to be and how strong it needs to be and where to place pump stations to add additional energy where it is needed. Then these are checked to be sure they fit proper design procedures. I then size the components in accordance with accepted practice to produce the desired result. Then I set up the construction specifications again in accordance with accepted practices and have it built. Finally, we test out the system to be sure it all works as intended and turn on the switch to start it up. What a feeling of joy and accomplishment I experience when I see it all working is intended. All the independent components pipe, motors, pumps, and electrical controls all come together in harmony to produce the desired result. Sad to say my work is not perfect as the Lord's because all things man puts together has flaws that we can't detect and control. Consider how God felt when the following statements were made:

GENESIS 1:9-12 KING JAMES VERSION (KJV)
9 And God said, Let the waters under the heaven be gathered
together unto one place, and let the dry land appear: and it was so.

¹⁰ And God called the dry land Earth; and the gathering together of the waters called he Seas: and God saw that it was good.

¹¹ And God said, Let the earth bring forth grass, the herb yielding seed, and the fruit tree yielding fruit after his kind, whose seed is in itself, upon the earth: and it was so.

¹² And the earth brought forth grass, and herb yielding seed after his kind, and the tree yielding fruit, whose seed was in itself, after his kind: and God saw that it was good.

God did not have guidelines to go by or a set of codes and standards which He had to follow. He was the initial and final authority in all that He did when He made creation. See Job chapters 37-42. There are so many scriptures which detail how He needed no counsel or guidance when He created the universe.

JOB 40:1-24 AMPLIFIED BIBLE (AMP)

Job: What Can I Say?

¹ Then the Lord said to Job,

² "Will the faultfinder contend with the Almighty? Let him who disputes with God answer it."

³ Then Job replied to the Lord and said,

⁴ "Behold, I am of little importance and contemptible; what can I reply to You? I lay my hand on my mouth.

⁵ "I have spoken once, but I will not reply again—Indeed, twice [I have answered], and I will add nothing further." God Questions Job

⁶ Then the Lord answered Job out of the whirlwind, saying,

⁷ "Now [a]gird up your loins (prepare yourself) like a man, And I will ask you, and you instruct Me.

⁸ "Will you really annul My judgment and set it aside as void? Will you condemn Me [your God] that you may [appear to] be righteous and justified?

⁹ "Have you an arm like God, And can you thunder with a voice like His?

¹⁰ "Adorn yourself with eminence and dignity [since you question the Almighty], And array yourself with honor and majesty.

¹¹ "Pour out the overflowings of your wrath, And look at everyone who is proud and make him low.

¹² Look at everyone who is proud, and humble him, And [if you are so able] tread down the wicked where they stand.

¹³ "[Crush and] hide them in the dust together; Shut them up in the hidden place [the house of death].

[14] *"[If you can do all this, Job, proving your divine power] then I [God] will also praise you and acknowledge That your own right hand can save you. God's Power Shown in Creatures*

[15] *"Behold now, [b]Behemoth, which I created as well as you; He eats grass like an ox.*

[16] *"See now, his strength is in his loins And his power is in the muscles and sinews of his belly.*

[17] *"He sways his tail like a cedar; The tendons of his thighs are twisted and knit together [like a rope].*

[18] *"His bones are tubes of bronze; His [c]limbs are like bars of iron.*

[19] *"He is the first [in magnitude and power] of the works of God; [Only] He who made him can bring near His sword [to master him].*

[20] *"Surely the mountains bring him food, And all the wild animals play there.*

[21] *"He lies down under the lotus plants, In the hidden shelter of the reeds in the marsh.*

[22] *"The lotus plants cover him with their shade; The willows of the brook surround him.*

[23] *"If a river rages and overflows, he does not tremble; He is confident, though the Jordan [River] swells and rushes against his mouth.*

[24] *"Can anyone capture him when he is on watch, Or pierce his nose with barbs [to trap him]?*

FOOTNOTES:

Job 40:7 See note 38:3.

Job 40:15 Or the hippopotamus. Although Behemoth cannot be identified with certainty, the biblical description seems most like the hippopotamus. In ancient times it may have been even more formidable than today. In Job's day the hippopotamus was the largest known creature, was commonly found in the lower Nile River, and may also have existed in the Jordan.

Job 40:18 Lit bones.

JOB 42:1-6 AMPLIFIED BIBLE (AMP)

Job's Confession

[1] *Then Job answered the Lord and said,*

[2] *"I know that You can do all things, And that no thought or purpose of Yours can be restrained.*

[3] *"[You said to me] 'Who is this that darkens and obscures counsel [by words] without knowledge?' Therefore [I now see] I have [rashly] uttered that which I did not understand, Things too wonderful for me, which I did not know.*

> *4 'Hear, please, and I will speak; I will ask You, and You instruct [and answer] me.'*
> *5 "I had heard of You [only] by the hearing of the ear, But now my [spiritual] eye sees You.*
> *6 "Therefore I retract [my words and hate myself] And I repent in dust and ashes."*

All of our scientific knowledge comes as a result of our observation of how the elements in the universe function. We have found there are rules in place that each part of the creation follows so we try to observe how these are organized. We put together mathematical expressions to duplicate these and are careful to point out the inherent limitations.

A lot of our scientific discoveries came about not by our intelligent effort but many times by accident. Consider the discovery of penicillin. It was discovered by accident in a lab experiment. To me this is an indicator of a creator providing help to those who are unable to have the necessary faith in Him. To me it is just as He did with the people of Israel in the desert when they wanted help prevent death from snake bites. God gave them a serpent on a pole as a sign for their healing. Here we can see that He wants us to be healed from disease.

> ### NUMBERS 21:7-9 KING JAMES VERSION (KJV)
> *7 Therefore the people came to Moses, and said, We have sinned, for we have spoken against the Lord, and against thee; pray unto the Lord, that he take away the serpents from us. And Moses prayed for the people.*
> *8 And the Lord said unto Moses, Make thee a fiery serpent, and set it upon a pole: and it shall come to pass, that every one that is bitten, when he looketh upon it, shall live.*
> *9 And Moses made a serpent of brass, and put it upon a pole, and it came to pass, that if a serpent had bitten any man, when he beheld the serpent of brass, he lived.*

Conclusion

So, who are we to question whether the tenets of God or right or wrong? Is it not enough that we accept them? He more than anyone knows His creation. He understands man's inner workings. He knows what makes us tick so to speak. He understands what influences us or what does not. Just as God understands the workings and design parameters (the laws which govern their operation of each element) He used when He made the universe. He has complete understanding of how man goes about making decisions and making evaluations. He has provided a list of ways we can produce error and not accomplish that for which we were created. So, He set up a system of commandments for us to prevent us from harming each other and not being able to perform the purpose for which we were created. When we go against God's commandments, He takes on the role of making the necessary correction to bring things back in balance.

GENESIS 5:1-3 KING JAMES VERSION (KJV)
¹ This is the book of the generations of Adam. In the day that God created man, in the likeness of God made he him;
² Male and female created he them; and blessed them, and called their name Adam, in the day when they were created.
³ And Adam lived an hundred and thirty years, and begat a son in his own likeness, and after his image; and called his name Seth:

ISAIAH 42:4-5 KING JAMES VERSION (KJV)
⁴ He shall not fail nor be discouraged, till he have set judgment in the earth: and the isles shall wait for his law.
⁵ Thus saith God the Lord, he that created the heavens, and stretched them out; he that spread forth the earth, and that which cometh out of it; he that giveth breath unto the people upon it, and spirit to them that walk therein:

ISAIAH 45:17-19 KING JAMES VERSION (KJV)
¹⁷ But Israel shall be saved in the Lord with an everlasting salvation: ye shall not be ashamed nor confounded world without end.
¹⁸ For thus saith the Lord that created the heavens; God himself that formed the earth and made it; he hath established it, he created it not in vain, he formed it to be inhabited: I am the Lord; and there is none else.
¹⁹ I have not spoken in secret, in a dark place of the earth: I said not unto the seed of Jacob, Seek ye me in vain: I the Lord speak righteousness, I declare things that are right.

Yes, He knows the limits we have to stay within to be His original design for man. When we work outside these bounds then trouble results.

One last item. Not only did God grant us the ability to choose between right and wrong He first placed in us the ability to understand what is right and what is wrong. Scripture states God has placed within man a mechanism whereby he has the ability to know right and wrong. See the following:

LUKE 12:56-58 AMPLIFIED BIBLE (AMP)

[56] You hypocrites (play-actors, pretenders)! You know how to analyze and intelligently interpret the appearance of the earth and sky [to forecast the weather], but why do you not intelligently interpret this present time?

[57] "And why do you not even on your own initiative judge what is right?

[58] For while you are going with your opponent [at law] to appear before a magistrate, on the way make an effort to settle, so that he does not drag you before the judge, and the judge does not [rule against you and] turn you over to the officer, and the officer does not throw you into prison.

LUKE 19:21-23 KING JAMES VERSION (KJV)

[21] For I feared thee, because thou art an austere man: thou takest up that thou layedst not down, and reapest that thou didst not sow.

[22] And he saith unto him, Out of thine own mouth will I judge thee, thou wicked servant. Thou knewest that I was an austere man, taking up that I laid not down, and reaping that I did not sow:

[23] Wherefore then gavest not thou my money into the bank, that at my coming I might have required mine own with usury?

ACTS 13:45-47 KING JAMES VERSION (KJV)

[45] But when the Jews saw the multitudes, they were filled with envy, and spake against those things which were spoken by Paul, contradicting and blaspheming.

[46] Then Paul and Barnabas waxed bold, and said, It was necessary that the word of God should first have been spoken to you: but seeing ye put it from you, and judge yourselves unworthy of everlasting life, lo, we turn to the Gentiles.

[47] For so hath the Lord commanded us, saying, I have set thee to be a light of the Gentiles, that thou shouldest be for salvation unto the ends of the earth.

MATTHEW 12:33-35 KING JAMES VERSION (KJV)

[33] Either make the tree good, and his fruit good; or else make the tree corrupt, and his fruit corrupt: for the tree is known by his fruit.

[34] O generation of vipers, how can ye, being evil, speak good things? for out of the abundance of the heart the mouth speaketh.

[35] A good man out of the good treasure of the heart bringeth forth good things: and an evil man out of the evil treasure bringeth forth evil things.

MATTHEW 15:18-20 KING JAMES VERSION (KJV)
18 But those things which proceed out of the mouth come forth from the heart; and they defile the man.
19 For out of the heart proceed evil thoughts, murders, adulteries, fornications, thefts, false witness, blasphemies:
20 These are the things which defile a man: but to eat with unwashen hands defileth not a man.

1 TIMOTHY 1:4-6 KING JAMES VERSION (KJV)
4 Neither give heed to fables and endless genealogies, which minister questions, rather than godly edifying which is in faith: so do.
5 Now the end of the commandment is charity out of a pure heart, and of a good conscience, and of faith unfeigned:
6 From which some having swerved have turned aside unto vain jangling;

ROMANS 2:14-16 KING JAMES VERSION (KJV)
14 For when the Gentiles, which have not the law, do by nature the things contained in the law, these, having not the law, are a law unto themselves:
15 Which shew the work of the law written in their hearts, their conscience also bearing witness, and their thoughts the mean while accusing or else excusing one another;)
16 In the day when God shall judge the secrets of men by Jesus Christ according to my gospel.

ROMANS 2:14-16 AMPLIFIED BIBLE, CLASSIC EDITION (AMPC)
14 When Gentiles who have not the [divine] Law do instinctively what the Law requires, they are a law to themselves, since they do not have the Law.
15 They show that the essential requirements of the Law are written in their hearts and are operating there, with which their consciences (sense of right and wrong) also bear witness; and their [moral] [a]decisions (their arguments of reason, their condemning or approving [b]thoughts) will accuse or perhaps defend and excuse [them]
16 On that day when, as my Gospel proclaims, God by Jesus Christ will judge men in regard to [c]the things which they conceal (their hidden thoughts).

FOOTNOTES:
Romans 2:15 Joseph Thayer, A Greek-English Lexicon of the New Testament.
Romans 2:15 Henry Alford, The Greek New Testament, with Notes.
Romans 2:16 Henry Alford, The Greek New Testament, with Notes.

So, as the book of Romans states each man has the law (the knowledge of good and evil) written in both his inner being (heart and conscience) and it is by these men are judged.

CHAPTER 4

Reverence

T he act of reverence is something we in this country have a difficult time understanding. We are taught that we are free to do whatever we want when we want as long as we can get away with it. We are told we are just as good as the next guy and we all have the opportunity to get rich. The goal used to be for us to have our two cars in the driveway and two chickens in the pot. Now, it is getting all we can while we can, what we revere is wealth and power. Is this not part of the trend to complete one's bucket list before we die? Of course, there is the other end of the spectrum where those born in the welfare system are influenced to stay that way and allow the government to be their keeper. This is a form of economic slavery. Which, from what I have found, was the original intent of the welfare system. No matter which end of the spectrum we find ourselves in, our economy is based on the rich becoming richer and the poor becoming poorer. It is all driven by the Me, My, Mine mentality. It is the "me first" above all else syndrome and as scripture terms it; it is the lust within us. Well, before I go further, let us consider what reverence is.

Reverence has to do with respect in biblical terms. Respect for the position someone holds or respect for and individual for his or her outstanding qualities. Now this depends on what our frame of reference is. Man has his guidelines and God has a different set. Some of these are close but most are far afield. When it comes to appreciating royalty, many see the queen and king of England and other monarchs. Some are drawn to the pomp and circumstance that they abide in. Others are drawn to the absolute dictator and how they gain reverence through force and the use of power and use of the element of fear.

Man's view point may also have to do with strength or the fact that we see someone as smarter than ourselves or richer or more notable than us. Darwin's view of survival of the fittest is prominent in the way some see reverence. Many view the more powerful as deserving more respect or are to be feared. Fear in this since is considered as being placed on a pedestal. This can be based on a man's strength, size or wealth. Or, as stated above, the fact someone is smarter due to the title in their name. Just as the title PHD in a person's name is supposed to be a symbol of a person's expertise and their higher degree of understanding and intelligence. You see this expressed very succinctly in the educational community. The ability of one man to exercise control over others is what we see as reverence. I know for most of my life this how I've viewed it. It, for some us, is the start of the worship of man. Here is the essence of man's issue, the powerful want to be feared. They want to be reverenced. They want to be idolized. Some want to take it to the point where they wish to be considered as gods. Case in point, the Roman emperors went from being presented as rulers to wanting to be considered and revered as gods.

Consider the cast system in some societies. It is used as a way of relegating individuals as a higher estate than those of others. Those of lower estate are to look up to or revere those of higher estate and those of lower estate are considered to have less value or worth. In the United States the level which you are in can be determined by either your wealth or your educational level or fame, such as celebrities. Many today worship certain stars and musicians. Need I not also add race or nationality as part of the defining link in cast identity? For many the Eugenics movement was and still is practiced. It is based on the theory that physical, medical and mental abnormalities should be bred out of society so only those with better genes survive. Race was also included in this movement. This movement and its evil were initiated in the United States and was brought to prominence by Hitler through his promotion of the so-called "master race." Many still support it through demands that people be sterilized to prevent propagating bad genes. Many criminals today are being considered as needing to be castrated or sterilized to prevent propagation of their kind. Many movements also use Eugenics as a basis for their beliefs and platforms. Now doctors are also joining the fray by the use of gene therapy and manipulation to weed out not only disease but also those bad traits in man.

In the past when I read the words "fear the Lord" in the bible the image invoked was to be afraid. This is because in my life this has been how the word fear had always been used. The dimension of the word "fear" meaning respect is a more recent concept for me. Most of the time the meaning of unfamiliar words is determined by the way they are used in a sentence. Most of the time words are interpreted based on the way they are used in common everyday speech. Unlike some who will run to a dictionary to determine the meaning of words, I stay with modern day usage of words. Like many I have never been one who is a word smith. We have to remember that the most commonly used bible was written in the King James English and many words had different meanings at that time. We also in this day and time have come to understand that even today the meaning of words changes and continue to change based on common usage. The usage of many words doesn't even at times relate to their original meaning.

The Spirit wants me to direct you to see what scripture has to say. First it is the fact that we need to know who God is and what there is about him that points us to revere Him.

Scripture first of all points out that God is love. He loves with a pure love and there is nothing in Him that love doesn't touch. It drives all that He is and all that He does.

DEUTERONOMY 7:8-10 KING JAMES VERSION (KJV)

8 But because the Lord loved you, and because he would keep the oath which he had sworn unto your fathers, hath the Lord brought you out with a mighty hand, and redeemed you out of the house of bondmen, from the hand of Pharaoh king of Egypt.

9 Know therefore that the Lord thy God, he is God, the faithful God, which keepeth covenant and mercy with them that love him and keep his commandments to a thousand generations;

10 And repayeth them that hate him to their face, to destroy them: he will not be slack to him that hateth him, he will repay him to his face.

ROMANS 8:38-39 KING JAMES VERSION (KJV)

38 For I am persuaded, that neither death, nor life, nor angels, nor principalities, nor powers, nor things present, nor things to come,

39 Nor height, nor depth, nor any other creature, shall be able to separate us from the love of God, which is in Christ Jesus our Lord.

1 JOHN 4:6-9 KING JAMES VERSION (KJV)

6 We are of God: he that knoweth God heareth us; he that is not of God heareth not us. Hereby know we the spirit of truth, and the spirit of error.

7 Beloved, let us love one another: for love is of God; and every one that loveth is born of God, and knoweth God.

8 He that loveth not knoweth not God; for God is love.

9 In this was manifested the love of God toward us, because that God sent his only begotten Son into the world, that we might live through him.

PSALM 45:6-8 KING JAMES VERSION (KJV)

6 Thy throne, O God, is for ever and ever: the sceptre of thy kingdom is a right sceptre.

7 Thou lovest righteousness, and hatest wickedness: therefore God, thy God, hath anointed thee with the oil of gladness above thy fellows.

8 All thy garments smell of myrrh, and aloes, and cassia, out of the ivory palaces, whereby they have made thee glad.

JOHN 3:15-17 KING JAMES VERSION (KJV)

15 That whosoever believeth in him should not perish, but have eternal life.

16 For God so loved the world, that he gave his only begotten Son, that whosoever believeth in him should not perish, but have everlasting life.

17 For God sent not his Son into the world to condemn the world; but that the world through him might be saved.

JOHN 16:26-28 KING JAMES VERSION (KJV)

26 At that day ye shall ask in my name: and I say not unto you, that I will pray the Father for you:

27 For the Father himself loveth you, because ye have loved me, and have believed that I came out from God.

28 I came forth from the Father, and am come into the world: again, I leave the world, and go to the Father.

ROMANS 5:7-9 KING JAMES VERSION (KJV)

7 For scarcely for a righteous man will one die: yet peradventure for a good man some would even dare to die.

8 But God commendeth his love toward us, in that, while we were yet sinners, Christ died for us.

9 Much more then, being now justified by his blood, we shall be saved from wrath through him.

2 CORINTHIANS 13:10-12 KING JAMES VERSION (KJV)

[10] *Therefore I write these things being absent, lest being present I should use sharpness, according to the power which the Lord hath given me to edification, and not to destruction.*

[11] *Finally, brethren, farewell. Be perfect, be of good comfort, be of one mind, live in peace; and the God of love and peace shall be with you.*

[12] *Greet one another with an holy kiss.*

GALATIANS 2:19-21 KING JAMES VERSION (KJV)

[19] *For I through the law am dead to the law, that I might live unto God.*

[20] *I am crucified with Christ: nevertheless I live; yet not I, but Christ liveth in me: and the life which I now live in the flesh I live by the faith of the Son of God, who loved me, and gave himself for me.*

[21] *I do not frustrate the grace of God: for if righteousness come by the law, then Christ is dead in vain.*

EPHESIANS 2:3-5 KING JAMES VERSION (KJV)

[3] *Among whom also we all had our conversation in times past in the lusts of our flesh, fulfilling the desires of the flesh and of the mind; and were by nature the children of wrath, even as others.*

[4] *But God, who is rich in mercy, for his great love wherewith he loved us,*

[5] *Even when we were dead in sins, hath quickened us together with Christ, (by grace ye are saved;)*

EPHESIANS 3:18-20 KING JAMES VERSION (KJV)

[18] *May be able to comprehend with all saints what is the breadth, and length, and depth, and height;*

[19] *And to know the love of Christ, which passeth knowledge, that ye might be filled with all the fulness of God.*

[20] *Now unto him that is able to do exceeding abundantly above all that we ask or think, according to the power that worketh in us,*

1 THESSALONIANS 4:8-10 KING JAMES VERSION (KJV)

[8] *He therefore that despiseth, despiseth not man, but God, who hath also given unto us his holy Spirit.*

[9] *But as touching brotherly love ye need not that I write unto you: for ye yourselves are taught of God to love one another.*

[10] *And indeed ye do it toward all the brethren which are in all Macedonia: but we beseech you, brethren, that ye increase more and more;*

2 THESSALONIANS 2:15-17 KING JAMES VERSION (KJV)

[15] *Therefore, brethren, stand fast, and hold the traditions which ye have been taught, whether by word, or our epistle.*

[16] *Now our Lord Jesus Christ himself, and God, even our Father, which hath loved us, and hath given us everlasting consolation and good hope through grace,*

[17] *Comfort your hearts, and stablish you in every good word and work.*

1 TIMOTHY 6:10-12 KING JAMES VERSION (KJV)

[10] *For the love of money is the root of all evil: which while some coveted after, they have erred from the faith, and pierced themselves through with many sorrows.*

[11] *But thou, O man of God, flee these things; and follow after righteousness, godliness, faith, love, patience, meekness.*

[12] *Fight the good fight of faith, lay hold on eternal life, whereunto thou art also called, and hast professed a good profession before many witnesses.*

HEBREWS 6:9-11 KING JAMES VERSION (KJV)

[9] *But, beloved, we are persuaded better things of you, and things that accompany salvation, though we thus speak.*

[10] *For God is not unrighteous to forget your work and labour of love, which ye have shewed toward his name, in that ye have ministered to the saints, and do minister.*

[11] *And we desire that every one of you do shew the same diligence to the full assurance of hope unto the end:*

1 JOHN 3:1-3 KING JAMES VERSION (KJV)

[1] *Behold, what manner of love the Father hath bestowed upon us, that we should be called the sons of God: therefore the world knoweth us not, because it knew him not.*

[2] *Beloved, now are we the sons of God, and it doth not yet appear what we shall be: but we know that, when he shall appear, we shall be like him; for we shall see him as he is.*

[3] *And every man that hath this hope in him purifieth himself, even as he is pure.*

God has authority over all things. He created everything and has determined the rules or laws which each part of the creation has to follow in order to accomplish the intent of its creation. He ordains leaders for good so He established judges in Israel. Israel was chosen to represent to the world what a nation under divine authority should look like and how we are to pay respect and give reverence and honor to a true ruler, God himself. Before Israel choose to have a king, God appointed a judge to administer the judgement of God for the people and to defend the people of God from harm from inside and out. God choose a judge of righteous character to be a representative of Him on earth. That does not mean that this individual always adhered to the laws God had established. This was an ordinary person chosen not as a ruler but an intermediary between God and man.

Man wanted a man whom they could say he is our earthly ruler so men told God they wanted an earthly king not Him. God warned them that an earthly king would cause them nothing but trouble so Israel choose to have an earthly king with all the problems that come with it. We do the same this very day.

JUDGES 2:15-17 KING JAMES VERSION (KJV)

15 Whithersoever they went out, the hand of the Lord was against them for evil, as the Lord had said, and as the Lord had sworn unto them: and they were greatly distressed.

16 Nevertheless the Lord raised up judges, which delivered them out of the hand of those that spoiled them.

17 And yet they would not hearken unto their judges, but they went a whoring after other gods, and bowed themselves unto them: they turned quickly out of the way which their fathers walked in, obeying the commandments of the Lord; but they did not so.

JUDGES 4:3-5 KING JAMES VERSION (KJV)

3 And the children of Israel cried unto the Lord: for he had nine hundred chariots of iron; and twenty years he mightily oppressed the children of Israel.

4 And Deborah, a prophetess, the wife of Lapidoth, she judged Israel at that time.

5 And she dwelt under the palm tree of Deborah between Ramah and Bethel in mount Ephraim: and the children of Israel came up to her for judgment.

DEUTERONOMY 17:14-20 KING JAMES VERSION (KJV)

14 When thou art come unto the land which the Lord thy God giveth thee, and shalt possess it, and shalt dwell therein, and shalt say, I will set a king over me, like as all the nations that are about me;

15 Thou shalt in any wise set him king over thee, whom the Lord thy God shall choose: one from among thy brethren shalt thou set king over thee: thou mayest not set a stranger over thee, which is not thy brother.

16 But he shall not multiply horses to himself, nor cause the people to return to Egypt, to the end that he should multiply horses: forasmuch as the Lord hath said unto you, Ye shall henceforth return no more that way.

17 Neither shall he multiply wives to himself, that his heart turn not away: neither shall he greatly multiply to himself silver and gold.

18 And it shall be, when he sitteth upon the throne of his kingdom, that he shall write him a copy of this law in a book out of that which is before the priests the Levites:

19 And it shall be with him, and he shall read therein all the days of his life: that he may learn to fear the Lord his God, to keep all the words of this law and these statutes, to do them:

20 That his heart be not lifted up above his brethren, and that he turn not aside from the commandment, to the right hand, or to the left: to the end that he may prolong his days in his kingdom, he, and his children, in the midst of Israel.

1 SAMUEL 8:10-22 KING JAMES VERSION (KJV)

10 And Samuel told all the words of the Lord unto the people that asked of him a king.

11 And he said, This will be the manner of the king that shall reign over you: He will take your sons, and appoint them for himself, for his chariots, and to be his horsemen; and some shall run before his chariots.

12 And he will appoint him captains over thousands, and captains over fifties; and will set them to ear his ground, and to reap his harvest, and to make his instruments of war, and instruments of his chariots.

13 And he will take your daughters to be confectionaries, and to be cooks, and to be bakers.

14 And he will take your fields, and your vineyards, and your oliveyards, even the best of them, and give them to his servants.

15 And he will take the tenth of your seed, and of your vineyards, and give to his officers, and to his servants.

16 And he will take your menservants, and your maidservants, and your goodliest young men, and your asses, and put them to his work.

17 He will take the tenth of your sheep: and ye shall be his servants.

18 And ye shall cry out in that day because of your king which ye shall have chosen you; and the Lord will not hear you in that day.

19 Nevertheless the people refused to obey the voice of Samuel; and they said, Nay; but we will have a king over us;

20 That we also may be like all the nations; and that our king may judge us, and go out before us, and fight our battles.

21 And Samuel heard all the words of the people, and he rehearsed them in the ears of the Lord.

22 And the Lord said to Samuel, Hearken unto their voice, and make them a king. And Samuel said unto the men of Israel, Go ye every man unto his city.

ROMANS 13:1 KING JAMES VERSION (KJV)
¹ Let every soul be subject unto the higher powers. For there is no power but of God: the powers that be are ordained of God.

Many misinterpret this scripture to mean that all powers are ordained of God. That is not what is being said here. It is only referencing the power of God himself no other.

Conclusion

- God is the creator.
- God is all powerful.
- Everything in the universe is God breathed and created.
- Nothing can exist without God.
- God owns it all.
- God does not force us to revere Him.
- He does not even force us to recognize His existence.
- We are to worship God only.
- The only true ordained power is from God above.

The rule of men has been corrupted by the thirst to gain more; more power; more money; more control; more fame; more of everything. They don't seem to understand that this existence and all our goods are all temporary and one day we will all die and none of this can be taken with us. The pharaohs tried this with the great pyramids and their tombs filled with riches. All that stuff stayed behind. The power that one man exerts over another is not what God wants or intends. God is to be worshipped and praised. Respect Him for He is our creator and the one by whom we live and move and have our being or existence. The value in our possessions only lies in the good for which they can be used to spread the kingdom of God and His righteousness.

ACTS 17:27-29 KING JAMES VERSION (KJV)
²⁷ That they should seek the Lord, if haply they might feel after him, and find him, though he be not far from every one of us:
²⁸ For in him we live, and move, and have our being; as certain also of your own poets have said, For we are also his offspring.
²⁹ Forasmuch then as we are the offspring of God, we ought not to think that the Godhead is like unto gold, or silver, or stone, graven by art and man's device.

MARK 10:21-23 KING JAMES VERSION (KJV)

[21] *Then Jesus beholding him loved him, and said unto him, One thing thou lackest: go thy way, sell whatsoever thou hast, and give to the poor, and thou shalt have treasure in heaven: and come, take up the cross, and follow me.*

[22] *And he was sad at that saying, and went away grieved: for he had great possessions.*

[23] *And Jesus looked round about, and saith unto his disciples, How hardly shall they that have riches enter into the kingdom of God!*

ACTS 2:44-46 KING JAMES VERSION (KJV)

[44] *And all that believed were together, and had all things common;*

[45] *And sold their possessions and goods, and parted them to all men, as every man had need.*

[46] *And they, continuing daily with one accord in the temple, and breaking bread from house to house, did eat their meat with gladness and singleness of heart,*

CHAPTER 5

Grace

Grace is a most interesting concept. It carries with it many connotations. The closest thing we can come to it in human terms is the term to pardon someone for the commission of a crime. Even though an individual is granted a Pardon there are lifelong impacts from those wrong choices which are not erased. Godly grace is so much different in that it does not mean man can escape the earthly results or consequences for his choices. Let's reason through this together.

As I watched the testimony of a victim of the crime of rape yesterday, I began to understand the need for grace. First of all, we cannot always comprehend the impact of our sin on others. This person related how the act will impact her for her entire life. The mental scars left behind are such that no band aid, ointment or amount of counseling can heal or remove them. No apology or no degree of sorrow for what she experienced can heal these wounds. An apology may or may not open the door for healing. Neither can it undo the act or the experience. All an apology can do is make an admission that what was done was wrong and expose the perpetrator. It does not punish the wrong doer nor does it bring restitution for the crime or sin. It does not necessarily resolve the emotional and psychological damage that has occurred. Only the Holy Spirit can do this. Yes, confession does help resolve the person's desire for justice but it does not heal the soul. In this case she received no confession so she received no consolation at all. She was ridiculed by others for her admission adding insult to injury. This is the typical response women receive in this circumstance.

My spirit was pierced. I could see that I myself have done similar things in my life. Even though I escaped punishment at times, my victims had not. They are still being punished by the things I did and no amount of saying I am sorry can remove this from their lives even though I may have thoughts of how wrong what I did was. It cannot erase the past and it cannot undo the wrong. My understanding of my wrong does not even come close to the impact it has had on those innocent victims. Many times, in my sermons, I have stated that there are things which I have done for which I should have been thrown under the jail for. I do not enumerate the details which I believe only glorifies the act and I am afraid of how others will view me. Those who hear this say well, it could not be that bad, but, yes, it is. I know many times I have confessed how I as a child would steal money from my mom's purse so that I could buy candy. At the time I did not understand that I was taking her bus fare so she had to walk to work in the snow or rain or cold and then put in a full day's work. Some see this as childish, but do you see the pain and suffering it caused my mom who had bad feet and the pain she had to endure. I did not consider how it hurt her to know how she was sacrificing every little penny to help provide us with food and shelter. What about the disappointment she had in knowing someone she loved so dearly would do such harm to her? You may see this as a minor issue but it was much, much, more. Yes, using terms I grew up with, I skated by or dodged the bullet or escaped my well-deserved punishment. Yet my mom carried these scars all her life but for me I only had a brief feeling of guilt. By the way, I never told her about what I had done but, somehow, I feel she knew. So, because I escaped earthly punishment, do you think I will escape eternal judgment without the shed blood of Christ Jesus. We don't understand how far reaching the sin we have done is or the degree of impact it has. What made me stop doing this was that one day I was almost caught but not punished because she pretended not to know what I was doing. From then on, the fear that I would be punished stopped me from doing this again. The fear of being discovered has been my stopping point in many situations. Maybe, just maybe, it is also the knowledge that sin is wrong that stops me in my tracks. Or as scripture states, each man has built in his conscience the knowledge of right and wrong. Is that what stopped me? Or could it have been those weekly sermons which stuck in my memory as though they had been branded in my mind.

HEBREWS 5:13-14 KING JAMES VERSION (KJV)
¹³ For every one that useth milk is unskilful in the word of righteousness: for he is a babe.
¹⁴ But strong meat belongeth to them that are of full age, even those who by reason of use have their senses exercised to discern both good and evil.

ROMANS 2:14-16 KING JAMES VERSION (KJV)
¹⁴ For when the Gentiles, which have not the law, do by nature the things contained in the law, these, having not the law, are a law unto themselves:
¹⁵ Which shew the work of the law written in their hearts, their conscience also bearing witness, and their thoughts the mean while accusing or else excusing one another;)
¹⁶ In the day when God shall judge the secrets of men by Jesus Christ according to my gospel.

2 CORINTHIANS 4:1-3 KING JAMES VERSION (KJV)
¹ Therefore seeing we have this ministry, as we have received mercy, we faint not;
² But have renounced the hidden things of dishonesty, not walking in craftiness, nor handling the word of God deceitfully; but by manifestation of the truth commending ourselves to every man's conscience in the sight of God.
³ But if our gospel be hid, it is hid to them that are lost:

So how does grace enter the equation here? First God knows my sin. We should not be like those in Israel who felt that they could receive restitution for their acts of sin by having an animal killed and offered to God for this. There is no temple in Jerusalem that I can go to the priest to offer up a sacrifice for me to God. So where and how does the grace of God come into the equation. It starts with repentance after responding to the Holy Spirit. This is more than saying I am sorry for what I did. It has definite pattern or set law that God has prescribed. The steps are:

1. Recognize that God is the only God and that in Jesus the Christ we have both a sacrifice for our sin and reconciliation to God through Him and the Holy Spirit.
2. Jesus is both our sacrifice and our High priest which stands between us and God to bring an acceptable offering.
3. Admit and reconcile.

4. Recognize the wrong done. Look at sin as sin. The greatest sin is not recognizing the true God as our creator and we should follow Him.
5. Identify that what you are doing is wrong.
6. If possible, make restitution for the wrong done. If this requires going to jail, so be it. This is the sign that I have received true Godly love in my heart.
7. Ask God for forgiveness based on the sacrifice performed by Jesus of Nazareth.
8. Receive the offering of Jesus and His offer to eternal life and accepting His sacrifice for your eternal punishment.
9. Denounce this sin and do it no more.
10. Be baptized and be obedient to His commandments that His Spirit may be with us.

These steps are very similar to what you find in the twelve-step program for the Alcoholics anonymous program which was originally based on scripture. I believe its success has been watered down by leaving God's love for us and our love for others out of the process which is the true reason for change.

Now back to the grace of God. His grace is demonstrated by Him blotting this sin from our book of life and accepting the punishment Jesus performed on the cross as payment for our sin. Most of us don't understand that sin carries with it both earthly and eternal consequences. Just as Jesus' sacrifice for sin carried both earthly and heavenly consequences. Though God grants heavenly forgiveness, we must try to rectify here on earth what we have done. This is the act of us truly loving our neighbor just as God loves us. It is just as scripture describes that we must repay the money or goods we have stolen to the rightful owner. This is an earthly demonstration that we have accepted God's love and are willing to demonstrate this same love to others. There are some things which we can never repay or make restitution for. But we must try. We cannot repair the damage done to those who have suffered mental anguish from our actions. That, only the Holy Spirit can only do. The goal is to have heaven on earth. This is a display to all that we are truly repentant and that we truly have had a change of heart and demonstrates to others they should do the same. It also brings to the forefront that sin is destructive and that I can no longer be used or bribed to hide it.

LEVITICUS 6:4-6 KING JAMES VERSION (KJV)
4 Then it shall be, because he hath sinned, and is guilty, that he shall restore that which he took violently away, or the thing which he hath deceitfully gotten, or that which was delivered him to keep, or the lost thing which he found,
5 Or all that about which he hath sworn falsely; he shall even restore it in the principal, and shall add the fifth part more thereto, and give it unto him to whom it appertaineth, in the day of his trespass offering.
6 And he shall bring his trespass offering unto the Lord, a ram without blemish out of the flock, with thy estimation, for a trespass offering, unto the priest:

HOSEA 4:1-3 AMPLIFIED BIBLE (AMP)
God's Controversy with Israel
1 Hear the word of the Lord, you children of Israel,
For the Lord has a [legal] case with the inhabitants of the land,
Because there is no faithfulness [no steadfast love, no dependability] or loyalty or kindness
Or knowledge of God [from personal experience with Him] in the land.
2 There is [false] swearing of oaths, deception (broken faith), murder, stealing, and adultery;
They employ violence, so that one [act of] bloodshed follows closely on another.
3 Therefore the land [continually] mourns,
And everyone who lives in it languishes [in tragic suffering]
Together with the animals of the open country and the birds of the heavens;
Even the fish of the sea disappear.

Isn't the earth suffering today because of our abuse of the resources which God has provided? Pollution of the air and water. Using the natural resources as if they were only ours and not to be shared and without regard for the consequences. We shun the wisdom which we have seen from the past. We see it every day. The results of sin; thievery, lying, deception, unfaithfulness, continual bloodshed and loss of hope. We are killing ourselves and the world around us making life more difficult because of our greed and lust. I can vividly remember the attitude I had for so long from the statement (the solution to pollution is dilution). Yes, at one time I had no insight into the fact my attitude was all wrong.

MATTHEW 3:7-9 KING JAMES VERSION (KJV)

7 But when he saw many of the Pharisees and Sadducees come to his baptism, he said unto them, O generation of vipers, who hath warned you to flee from the wrath to come?

8 Bring forth therefore fruits meet for repentance:

9 And think not to say within yourselves, We have Abraham to our father: for I say unto you, that God is able of these stones to raise up children unto Abraham.

EPHESIANS 4:27-29 AMPLIFIED BIBLE (AMP)

27 And do not give the devil an opportunity [to lead you into sin by holding a grudge, or nurturing anger, or harboring resentment, or cultivating bitterness].

28 The thief [who has become a believer] must no longer steal, but instead he must work hard [making an honest living], producing that which is good with his own hands, so that he will have something to share with those in need.

29 Do not let unwholesome [foul, profane, worthless, vulgar] words ever come out of your mouth, but only such speech as is good for building up others, according to the need and the occasion, so that it will be a blessing to those who hear [you speak].

The words in the above scripture have been provided as instruction to the Christian community but it seems to have been ignored by many. Vulgar profane use of language is now seen as genuine expression and a way of showing how powerful we are or how real we are and in touch with the everyday man and woman. We need to see this is not so. It is the way the evil one keeps a hold on us by keeping us tied to the sin of the past. We need to cleanup this aspect of our lives to demonstrate the true impact of the gospel and the rejuvenating work of the Holy Spirit in our lives. There is no place in the house of God or in the lives of His people to use this form of speech. Scripture calls us to be clean in body, mind, spirit and speech.

ACTS 5:30-32 KING JAMES VERSION (KJV)

30 The God of our fathers raised up Jesus, whom ye slew and hanged on a tree.

31 Him hath God exalted with his right hand to be a Prince and a Saviour, for to give repentance to Israel, and forgiveness of sins.

32 And we are his witnesses of these things; and so is also the Holy Ghost, whom God hath given to them that obey him.

There are many today both in prison and out who believe that just by saying they are sorry they can be absolved of all punishment. This is not what the scripture declares and what God has taught. When there are fruits that demonstrate that true repentance has been done then He can forgive and His grace is shown. This He grants in water baptism as a symbol of His forgiveness and as a true act which has been shown by living a transformed life. Then He can grant the gift of eternal life and the Gift of the Holy Spirit to those who obey Him. Remember repentance starts with recognizing we have sinned (gone against the laws of God and that we are to demonstrate by what we do that we have changed from sinful lusts to those conducts as prescribed by His laws). It's just not done by reciting a few words. It has to carry more weight than that. Refer to chapter 8 on repentance.

Now Let's explore grace in the bible. Let's start with the slaying of Able by Cain. We see here where Cain is granted grace because God did not kill Cain or have him slain for murdering his brother. God did punish him by placing a mark on him to identify him as a murderer but prevented him from being killed by man for his deed. He paid for his sin on this earth by living a life of a marked man along with other judgements. He was imprisoned by his sin to demonstrate to the world God's dissatisfaction with sin and its destructive nature. Note Cain never confessed any sorrow for killing Able. He only confessed to doing the act because he had been caught.

> *GENESIS 4:9-17 KING JAMES VERSION (KJV)*
> *⁹ And the Lord said unto Cain, Where is Abel thy brother? And he said, I know not: Am I my brother's keeper?*
> *¹⁰ And he said, What hast thou done? the voice of thy brother's blood crieth unto me from the ground.*
> *¹¹ And now art thou cursed from the earth, which hath opened her mouth to receive thy brother's blood from thy hand;*
> *¹² When thou tillest the ground, it shall not henceforth yield unto thee her strength; a fugitive and a vagabond shalt thou be in the earth.*
> *¹³ And Cain said unto the Lord, My punishment is greater than I can bear.*
> *¹⁴ Behold, thou hast driven me out this day from the face of the earth; and from thy face shall I be hid; and I shall be a fugitive and a vagabond in the earth; and it shall come to pass, that every one that findeth me shall slay me.*
> *¹⁵ And the Lord said unto him, Therefore whosoever slayeth Cain, vengeance shall be taken on him sevenfold. And the Lord set a mark upon Cain, lest any finding him should kill him.*

16 And Cain went out from the presence of the Lord, and dwelt in the land of Nod, on the east of Eden.

17 And Cain knew his wife; and she conceived, and bare Enoch: and he builded a city, and called the name of the city, after the name of his son, Enoch.

Note that even though God provided His grace to Cain, Cain recognized he was also facing God's punishment here on earth.

There are many other instances such as these in the bible. Some of the more notable being Moses who killed the Egyptian and King David who had Uriah killed so that he would hide the sin of adultery with Uriah's wife. Both of them lived out the result of their sinful acts here on earth. Though God forgave them, they still in some way suffered the results of their sin here on earth.

EXODUS 2:13-15 KING JAMES VERSION (KJV)

13 And when he went out the second day, behold, two men of the Hebrews strove together: and he said to him that did the wrong, Wherefore smitest thou thy fellow?

14 And he said, Who made thee a prince and a judge over us? intendest thou to kill me, as thou killedst the Egyptian? And Moses feared, and said, Surely this thing is known.

15 Now when Pharaoh heard this thing, he sought to slay Moses. But Moses fled from the face of Pharaoh, and dwelt in the land of Midian: and he sat down by a well.

2 SAMUEL 11:2-4 KING JAMES VERSION (KJV)

2 And it came to pass in an eveningtide, that David arose from off his bed, and walked upon the roof of the king's house: and from the roof he saw a woman washing herself; and the woman was very beautiful to look upon.

3 And David sent and enquired after the woman. And one said, Is not this Bathsheba, the daughter of Eliam, the wife of Uriah the Hittite?

4 And David sent messengers, and took her; and she came in unto him, and he lay with her; for she was purified from her uncleanness: and she returned unto her house.

2 SAMUEL 12:8-10 KING JAMES VERSION (KJV)

8 And I gave thee thy master's house, and thy master's wives into thy bosom, and gave thee the house of Israel and of Judah; and if that had been too little, I would moreover have given unto thee such and such things.

9 Wherefore hast thou despised the commandment of the Lord, to do evil in his sight? thou hast killed Uriah the Hittite with the sword, and hast taken his wife to be thy wife, and hast slain him with the sword of the children of Ammon.

10 Now therefore the sword shall never depart from thine house; because thou hast despised me, and hast taken the wife of Uriah the Hittite to be thy wife.

King David did many things which under the Law of Moses for which he could have suffered death, but God's grace was extended to him. This is so that His grace as shown on multiple occasions for us to see His grace at work and that sin will carry consequences on this earth for us and those we know.

PROVERBS 3:33-35 KING JAMES VERSION (KJV)

33 The curse of the Lord is in the house of the wicked: but he blesseth the habitation of the just.

34 Surely he scorneth the scorners: but he giveth grace unto the lowly.

35 The wise shall inherit glory: but shame shall be the promotion of fools.

ACTS 15:10-12 KING JAMES VERSION (KJV)

10 Now therefore why tempt ye God, to put a yoke upon the neck of the disciples, which neither our fathers nor we were able to bear?

11 But we believe that through the grace of the Lord Jesus Christ we shall be saved, even as they.

12 Then all the multitude kept silence, and gave audience to Barnabas and Paul, declaring what miracles and wonders God had wrought among the Gentiles by them.

ACTS 20:31-33 KING JAMES VERSION (KJV)

31 Therefore watch, and remember, that by the space of three years I ceased not to warn every one night and day with tears.

32 And now, brethren, I commend you to God, and to the word of his grace, which is able to build you up, and to give you an inheritance among all them which are sanctified.

33 I have coveted no man's silver, or gold, or apparel.

ROMANS 3:23-25 KING JAMES VERSION (KJV)

23 For all have sinned, and come short of the glory of God;

24 Being justified freely by his grace through the redemption that is in Christ Jesus:

25 Whom God hath set forth to be a propitiation through faith in his blood, to declare his righteousness for the remission of sins that are past, through the forbearance of God;

ROMANS 5:16-18 KING JAMES VERSION (KJV)

[16] *And not as it was by one that sinned, so is the gift: for the judgment was by one to condemnation, but the free gift is of many offences unto justification.*

[17] *For if by one man's offence death reigned by one; much more they which receive abundance of grace and of the gift of righteousness shall reign in life by one, Jesus Christ.)*

[18] *Therefore as by the offence of one judgment came upon all men to condemnation; even so by the righteousness of one the free gift came upon all men unto justification of life.*

ROMANS 5:20-21 KING JAMES VERSION (KJV)

[20] *Moreover the law entered, that the offence might abound. But where sin abounded, grace did much more abound:*

[21] *That as sin hath reigned unto death, even so might grace reign through righteousness unto eternal life by Jesus Christ our Lord.*

ROMANS 6:14-16 KING JAMES VERSION (KJV)

[14] *For sin shall not have dominion over you: for ye are not under the law, but under grace.*

[15] *What then? shall we sin, because we are not under the law, but under grace? God forbid.*

[16] *Know ye not, that to whom ye yield yourselves servants to obey, his servants ye are to whom ye obey; whether of sin unto death, or of obedience unto righteousness?*

1 CORINTHIANS 15:9-11 KING JAMES VERSION (KJV)

[9] *For I am the least of the apostles, that am not meet to be called an apostle, because I persecuted the church of God.*

[10] *But by the grace of God I am what I am: and his grace which was bestowed upon me was not in vain; but I laboured more abundantly than they all: yet not I, but the grace of God which was with me.*

[11] *Therefore whether it were I or they, so we preach, and so ye believed.*

1 PETER 5:4-6 KING JAMES VERSION (KJV)

[4] *And when the chief Shepherd shall appear, ye shall receive a crown of glory that fadeth not away.*

[5] *Likewise, ye younger, submit yourselves unto the elder. Yea, all of you be subject one to another, and be clothed with humility: for God resisteth the proud, and giveth grace to the humble.*

[6] *Humble yourselves therefore under the mighty hand of God, that he may exalt you in due time:*

ISAIAH 61:1-11 KING JAMES VERSION (KJV)

[1] *The Spirit of the Lord God is upon me; because the Lord hath anointed me to preach good tidings unto the meek; he hath sent*

me to bind up the brokenhearted, to proclaim liberty to the captives, and the opening of the prison to them that are bound;

² To proclaim the acceptable year of the Lord, and the day of vengeance of our God; to comfort all that mourn;

³ To appoint unto them that mourn in Zion, to give unto them beauty for ashes, the oil of joy for mourning, the garment of praise for the spirit of heaviness; that they might be called trees of righteousness, the planting of the Lord, that he might be glorified.

⁴ And they shall build the old wastes, they shall raise up the former desolations, and they shall repair the waste cities, the desolations of many generations.

⁵ And strangers shall stand and feed your flocks, and the sons of the alien shall be your plowmen and your vinedressers.

⁶ But ye shall be named the Priests of the Lord: men shall call you the Ministers of our God: ye shall eat the riches of the Gentiles, and in their glory shall ye boast yourselves.

⁷ For your shame ye shall have double; and for confusion they shall rejoice in their portion: therefore in their land they shall possess the double: everlasting joy shall be unto them.

⁸ For I the Lord love judgment, I hate robbery for burnt offering; and I will direct their work in truth, and I will make an everlasting covenant with them.

⁹ And their seed shall be known among the Gentiles, and their offspring among the people: all that see them shall acknowledge them, that they are the seed which the Lord hath blessed.

¹⁰ I will greatly rejoice in the Lord, my soul shall be joyful in my God; for he hath clothed me with the garments of salvation, he hath covered me with the robe of righteousness, as a bridegroom decketh himself with ornaments, and as a bride adorneth herself with her jewels.

¹¹ For as the earth bringeth forth her bud, and as the garden causeth the things that are sown in it to spring forth; so the Lord God will cause righteousness and praise to spring forth before all the nations.

Conclusion

Grace can provide everlasting forgiveness and even provide an avenue for repentance but it will not remove the need for an earthly resolve for sins which we commit. The expression of grace is seen as mercy, kindness, release from past sin, favor and much more. Each of us has to answer the call that Jesus presented when He commissioned His disciples to go unto all the world and baptize people in His name.

MARK 16:14-16 KING JAMES VERSION (KJV)

[14] Afterward he appeared unto the eleven as they sat at meat, and upbraided them with their unbelief and hardness of heart, because they believed not them which had seen him after he was risen.

[15] And he said unto them, Go ye into all the world, and preach the gospel to every creature.

[16] He that believeth and is baptized shall be saved; but he that believeth not shall be damned.

MATTHEW 3:10-12 KING JAMES VERSION (KJV)

[10] And now also the axe is laid unto the root of the trees: therefore every tree which bringeth not forth good fruit is hewn down, and cast into the fire.

[11] I indeed baptize you with water unto repentance. but he that cometh after me is mightier than I, whose shoes I am not worthy to bear: he shall baptize you with the Holy Ghost, and with fire:

[12] Whose fan is in his hand, and he will throughly purge his floor, and gather his wheat into the garner; but he will burn up the chaff with unquenchable fire.

MATTHEW 28:19-20 KING JAMES VERSION (KJV)

[19] Go ye therefore, and teach all nations, baptizing them in the name of the Father, and of the Son, and of the Holy Ghost:

[20] Teaching them to observe all things whatsoever I have commanded you: and, lo, I am with you always, even unto the end of the world. Amen.

ACTS 20:23-25 KING JAMES VERSION (KJV)

[23] Save that the Holy Ghost witnesseth in every city, saying that bonds and afflictions abide me.

[24] But none of these things move me, neither count I my life dear unto myself, so that I might finish my course with joy, and the ministry, which I have received of the Lord Jesus, to testify the gospel of the grace of God.

[25] And now, behold, I know that ye all, among whom I have gone preaching the kingdom of God, shall see my face no more.

MARK 1:6-15 KING JAMES VERSION (KJV)

[6] And John was clothed with camel's hair, and with a girdle of a skin about his loins; and he did eat locusts and wild honey;

[7] And preached, saying, There cometh one mightier than I after me, the latchet of whose shoes I am not worthy to stoop down and unloose.

⁸ I indeed have baptized you with water: but he shall baptize you with the Holy Ghost.

⁹ And it came to pass in those days, that Jesus came from Nazareth of Galilee, and was baptized of John in Jordan.

¹⁰ And straightway coming up out of the water, he saw the heavens opened, and the Spirit like a dove descending upon him:

¹¹ And there came a voice from heaven, saying, Thou art my beloved Son, in whom I am well pleased.

¹² And immediately the spirit driveth him into the wilderness.

¹³ And he was there in the wilderness forty days, tempted of Satan; and was with the wild beasts; and the angels ministered unto him.

¹⁴ Now after that John was put in prison, Jesus came into Galilee, preaching the gospel of the kingdom of God,

¹⁵ And saying, The time is fulfilled, and the kingdom of God is at hand: repent ye, and believe the gospel.

The grace of God is offered to all. It is a shame that not many recognize the fact that God by His grace has provided our very existence and allowed us the free will to choose or reject Him and His ways. Our willingness to obey is evidence that we believe. We can only receive the benefit of the Holy Spirit when we obey Him. Just as John the Baptist called the people of Israel to repent and be baptized and John told them that one greater than himself (Jesus) will come after him to baptize with fire and the Holy Ghost.

Even though many have not had the opportunity to accept Jesus the Christ in this life, all will be offered this opportunity just as was demonstrated by Jesus visiting and preaching to those who were in prison in the three days between his death and resurrection.

PROVERBS 3:33-35 KING JAMES VERSION (KJV)

³³ The curse of the Lord is in the house of the wicked: but he blesseth the habitation of the just.

³⁴ Surely he scorneth the scorners: but he giveth grace unto the lowly.

³⁵ The wise shall inherit glory: but shame shall be the promotion of fools.

1 PETER 3:17-22 KING JAMES VERSION (KJV)

¹⁷ For it is better, if the will of God be so, that ye suffer for well doing, than for evil doing.

¹⁸ For Christ also hath once suffered for sins, the just for the unjust, that he might bring us to God, being put to death in the flesh, but quickened by the Spirit:

¹⁹ By which also he went and preached unto the spirits in prison;

²⁰ Which sometime were disobedient, when once the longsuffering of God waited in the days of Noah, while the ark was a preparing, wherein few, that is, eight souls were saved by water.
²¹ The like figure whereunto even baptism doth also now save us (not the putting away of the filth of the flesh, but the answer of a good conscience toward God,) by the resurrection of Jesus Christ:
²² Who is gone into heaven, and is on the right hand of God; angels and authorities and powers being made subject unto him.
ROMANS 2:14-16 KING JAMES VERSION (KJV)
¹⁴ For when the Gentiles, which have not the law, do by nature the things contained in the law, these, having not the law, are a law unto themselves:
¹⁵ Which shew the work of the law written in their hearts, their conscience also bearing witness, and their thoughts the mean while accusing or else excusing one another;)
¹⁶ In the day when God shall judge the secrets of men by Jesus Christ according to my gospel.

This also demonstrates the fairness of God through His grace. God's grace in judgement is only limited by the intent of men's hearts. His grace is for all without limit. The only limitation is how we choose to obey the works He has embedded in our conscience. We have often heard it said that some have no conscience. No, it is they have chosen to be disobedient to their conscience and let evil prevail.

Many have tried to make the gospel appealing to men by hiding the parts we see as distasteful so that we have crippled the work of the Jesus the Christ. Repentance is more than reciting the sinner's prayer that we so often hear. It requires a change of heart and mind and a change in our relationship with the past admitting our sin, making restitution where possible and being baptized and being obedient to God's ways to receive the gift of forgiveness and life eternal through the sacrifice of Jesus the Christ. His mercy is not to allow us to hide our sin but to take responsibility for the sin committed and resolve what we are able to here on this earth in loving response for Him and our fellow man. This is our rendering of God's love for us through our demonstrating our love for others.

The mandate in scripture is, after baptism, for us to seek first the kingdom of God and His righteousness in our lives then all the things necessary for us to live will be provided for us. It requires us to pray and surrender to the Holy Spirit for Him to make the changes in us so that we can replicate the righteous behavior of God here on earth. It is similar to what Jesus did when He went into the desert for 40 days and nights fasting and praying for God's strength and support. Paul did something similar when he went off to Arabia prior to proceeding on his ministry. The Catholic church even to this day has its priest spend time in learning and prayer prior to proceeding into ministry. I discuss this a little more in my first book, "Formulas In The Scripture E = MC^2 The Key To Our Pentecost Experience."

GALATIANS 1:13-18 KING JAMES VERSION (KJV)

^{13} For ye have heard of my conversation in time past in the Jews' religion, how that beyond measure I persecuted the church of God, and wasted it:

^{14} And profited in the Jews' religion above many my equals in mine own nation, being more exceedingly zealous of the traditions of my fathers.

^{15} But when it pleased God, who separated me from my mother's womb, and called me by his grace,

^{16} To reveal his Son in me, that I might preach him among the heathen; immediately I conferred not with flesh and blood:

^{17} Neither went I up to Jerusalem to them which were apostles before me; but I went into Arabia, and returned again unto Damascus.

^{18} Then after three years I went up to Jerusalem to see Peter, and abode with him fifteen days.

MARK 1:9-14 KING JAMES VERSION (KJV)

^{9} And it came to pass in those days, that Jesus came from Nazareth of Galilee, and was baptized of John in Jordan.

^{10} And straightway coming up out of the water, he saw the heavens opened, and the Spirit like a dove descending upon him:

^{11} And there came a voice from heaven, saying, Thou art my beloved Son, in whom I am well pleased.

^{12} And immediately the spirit driveth him into the wilderness.

^{13} And he was there in the wilderness forty days, tempted of Satan; and was with the wild beasts; and the angels ministered unto him.

^{14} Now after that John was put in prison, Jesus came into Galilee, preaching the gospel of the kingdom of God, 9 And it came to pass in those days, that Jesus came from Nazareth of Galilee, and was baptized of John in Jordan.

God's grace is always there but He can't provide it until we have freely shown and allowed His Holy Spirit to bring true repentance in our lives. His grace is not there as an escape from punishment but an escape from the grasp of sin in our lives.

EPHESIANS 2:7-9 KING JAMES VERSION (KJV)

[7] *That in the ages to come he might shew the exceeding riches of his grace in his kindness toward us through Christ Jesus.*

[8] *For by grace are ye saved through faith; and that not of yourselves: it is the gift of God:*

[9] *Not of works, lest any man should boast.*

JOHN 1:15-17 KING JAMES VERSION (KJV)

[15] *John bare witness of him, and cried, saying, This was he of whom I spake, He that cometh after me is preferred before me: for he was before me.*

[16] *And of his fulness have all we received, and grace for grace.*

[17] *For the law was given by Moses, but grace and truth came by Jesus Christ.*

ACTS 11:22-24 KING JAMES VERSION (KJV)

[22] *Then tidings of these things came unto the ears of the church which was in Jerusalem: and they sent forth Barnabas, that he should go as far as Antioch.*

[23] *Who, when he came, and had seen the grace of God, was glad, and exhorted them all, that with purpose of heart they would cleave unto the Lord.*

[24] *For he was a good man, and full of the Holy Ghost and of faith: and much people was added unto the Lord.*

ACTS 20:31-33 KING JAMES VERSION (KJV)

[31] *Therefore watch, and remember, that by the space of three years I ceased not to warn every one night and day with tears.*

[32] *And now, brethren, I commend you to God, and to the word of his grace, which is able to build you up, and to give you an inheritance among all them which are sanctified.*

[33] *I have coveted no man's silver, or gold, or apparel.*

2 CORINTHIANS 6:1-3 KING JAMES VERSION (KJV)

[6] *We then, as workers together with him, beseech you also that ye receive not the grace of God in vain.*

[2] *(For he saith, I have heard thee in a time accepted, and in the day of salvation have I succoured thee: behold, now is the accepted time; behold, now is the day of salvation.)*

[3] *Giving no offence in any thing, that the ministry be not blamed:*

1 PETER 4:9-11 KING JAMES VERSION (KJV)

[9] *Use hospitality one to another without grudging.*

[10] *As every man hath received the gift, even so minister the same one to another, as good stewards of the manifold grace of God.*

11 If any man speak, let him speak as the oracles of God; if any man minister, let him do it as of the ability which God giveth: that God in all things may be glorified through Jesus Christ, to whom be praise and dominion for ever and ever. Amen.

JUDE 3-5 AMPLIFIED BIBLE (AMP)

3 Beloved, while I was making every effort to write you about our common salvation, I was compelled to write to you [urgently] appealing that you [a]fight strenuously for [the defense of] the faith which was once for all [b]handed down to the saints [the faith that is the sum of Christian belief that was given verbally to believers].

4 For certain people have crept in unnoticed [just as if they were sneaking in by a side door]. They are ungodly persons whose condemnation was predicted long ago, for they distort the grace of our God into decadence and immoral freedom [viewing it as an opportunity to do whatever they want], and deny and disown our only Master and Lord, Jesus Christ.

5 Now I want to remind you, although you are fully informed once for all, that [c]the Lord, after saving a people out of the land of Egypt, subsequently destroyed those who did not believe [who refused to trust and obey and rely on Him].

FOOTNOTES:

Jude 1:3 Lit contend earnestly.

Jude 1:3 There is no "secret knowledge" or "better way" or alternative belief system which God has revealed to some unique group or teacher. The truth is available to everyone.

Jude 1:5 Two early mss read Jesus.

Grace is the expression of God's love for us and is to be extended to others the same way we receive it from God.

CHAPTER 6

Our Pardon

God's pardon is an action plan. Just as any pardon it carries with it some conditions. It entails more than leaving you on your own to fend for yourself. It is a provision which allows us to be set free from the past and its hold on us. Scripture describes this as being set free from the sins of the past which bound us to unloving expressions of living our lives toward God and others. It is a provision for release from the prison in which sin confines us. It opens the doorway for us to be set free to function as God intended for us in the beginning. It provides the opportunity for us to fully function in the freedom God intended in the beginning. Sin can no longer hold us like a prisoner, shackle our spirit and prevent our growth or limit our potential due to its confining attributes. We become free to be able to do the good works that we were created for, free to express our sorrow for the sins committed, free to be able to make restitution to those we have injured, free to bring happiness and good will to others and ourselves, free to express love as God ordained it to be. We are free to begin life in a new God ordained way. It is a fresh start where we can do our best to live in the way God intended from the very beginning. It allows us to love with true Godly love not in the limited way we do now.

> **PSALM 146:1-10 KING JAMES VERSION (KJV)**
> **¹ Praise ye the Lord. Praise the Lord, O my soul.**
> **² While I live will I praise the Lord: I will sing praises unto my God while I have any being.**
> **³ Put not your trust in princes, nor in the son of man, in whom there is no help.**

4 His breath goeth forth, he returneth to his earth; in that very day his thoughts perish.

5 Happy is he that hath the God of Jacob for his help, whose hope is in the Lord his God:

6 Which made heaven, and earth, the sea, and all that therein is: which keepeth truth for ever:

7 Which executeth judgment for the oppressed: which giveth food to the hungry. The Lord looseth the prisoners:

8 The Lord openeth the eyes of the blind: the Lord raiseth them that are bowed down: the Lord loveth the righteous:

9 The Lord preserveth the strangers; he relieveth the fatherless and widow: but the way of the wicked he turneth upside down.

10 The Lord shall reign for ever, even thy God, O Zion, unto all generations. Praise ye the Lord.

ISAIAH 51:13-15 KING JAMES VERSION (KJV)

13 And forgettest the Lord thy maker, that hath stretched forth the heavens, and laid the foundations of the earth; and hast feared continually every day because of the fury of the oppressor, as if he were ready to destroy? and where is the fury of the oppressor?

14 The captive exile hasteneth that he may be loosed, and that he should not die in the pit, nor that his bread should fail.

15 But I am the Lord thy God, that divided the sea, whose waves roared: The Lord of hosts is his name.

JEREMIAH 15:10-11 AMPLIFIED BIBLE (AMP)

*10 Woe to me, my mother, that you have given birth to me
To be a man of strife and a man of contention to all the earth! I have not loaned, nor have men lent money to me, Yet everyone curses me.*

*11 The Lord said, "Surely [it will go well for Judah's obedient remnant for] I will set you free for good purposes; Surely [Jeremiah] I will [intercede for you with the enemy and I will] cause the enemy to plead with you [for help]
In a time of disaster and a time of distress.*

LUKE 4:17-19 AMPLIFIED BIBLE (AMP)

17 The scroll of the prophet Isaiah was handed to Him. He unrolled the scroll and found the place where it was written,

*18 "The Spirit of the Lord is upon Me (the Messiah),
Because He has anointed Me to preach the good news to the poor.
He has sent Me to announce release (pardon, forgiveness) to the captives,
And recovery of sight to the blind,*

To set free those who are oppressed (downtrodden, bruised, crushed by tragedy),
¹⁹ to proclaim the favorable year of the Lord [the day when salvation and the favor of God abound greatly]."
JOHN 8:31-32 KING JAMES VERSION (KJV)
³¹ Then said Jesus to those Jews which believed on him, If ye continue in my word, then are ye my disciples indeed;
³² And ye shall know the truth, and the truth shall make you free.
EPHESIANS 1:6-8 AMPLIFIED BIBLE (AMP)
⁶ to the praise of His glorious grace and favor, which He so freely bestowed on us in the Beloved [His Son, Jesus Christ].
⁷ In Him we have redemption [that is, our deliverance and salvation] through His blood, [which paid the penalty for our sin and resulted in] the forgiveness and complete pardon of our sin, in accordance with the riches of His grace
⁸ which He lavished on us. In all wisdom and understanding [with practical insight]

God's pardon and forgiveness takes affect when we, through repentance and the baptism of the water exhibit an initial step in His process of pardon. This He then seals through the baptism of the Holy Spirit taking upon Himself the responsibility for the work required for the change of our existing nature into Its intended form. We in and of ourselves cannot accomplish this renewal work. But we have to identify that our present way of living is wrong and out of kilter or not in compliance with God's plan for us. Our baptism identifies that we have willingly and knowingly acknowledged our need for help to be set free from the limitations and restrictions we experience when we are walking in sin. Baptism is our acceptance of His pardon and recognition of Him as our Creator, God and King. It allows Him to remove these shackles and open the doorway to the rejuvenation that His pardon can bring. It is a commitment to not return to this condition and His commitment to guide us to new and improved expressions of true love. It is the symbol that the stains which were once upon us as a result of sin can be washed away. It is the identification that His Spirit has touched us and we are responding. He has always wanted to bring about what is best for us and new ways in which we can receive these innovations. The baptisms are agreements, between you and God, in which He sets forth that He will do all that is needed for your new walk and He will take you as far as you are willing to go.

PSALM 25:10-12 KING JAMES VERSION (KJV)
[10] All the paths of the Lord are mercy and truth unto such as keep his covenant and his testimonies.
[11] For thy name's sake, O Lord, pardon mine iniquity; for it is great.
[12] What man is he that feareth the Lord? him shall he teach in the way that he shall choose.

ISAIAH 55:6-8 KING JAMES VERSION (KJV)
[6] Seek ye the Lord while he may be found, call ye upon him while he is near:
[7] Let the wicked forsake his way, and the unrighteous man his thoughts: and let him return unto the Lord, and he will have mercy upon him; and to our God, for he will abundantly pardon.
[8] For my thoughts are not your thoughts, neither are your ways my ways, saith the Lord.

LUKE 6:36-38 AMPLIFIED BIBLE (AMP)
[36] Be merciful (responsive, compassionate, tender) just as your [heavenly] Father is merciful.
[37] "[a]Do not judge [others self-righteously], and you will not be judged; do not condemn [others when you are guilty and unrepentant], and you will not be condemned [for your hypocrisy]; pardon [others when they truly repent and change], and you will be pardoned [when you truly repent and change].
[38] Give, and it will be given to you. They will pour into your lap a good measure—pressed down, shaken together, and running over [with no space left for more]. For with the standard of measurement you use [when you do good to others], it will be measured to you in return."

ROMANS 6:17-19 KING JAMES VERSION (KJV)
[17] But God be thanked, that ye were the servants of sin, but ye have obeyed from the heart that form of doctrine which was delivered you.
[18] Being then made free from sin, ye became the servants of righteousness.
[19] I speak after the manner of men because of the infirmity of your flesh: for as ye have yielded your members servants to uncleanness and to iniquity unto iniquity; even so now yield your members servants to righteousness unto holiness.

ROMANS 6:17-19 AMPLIFIED BIBLE (AMP)
[17] But thank God that though you were slaves of sin, you became obedient with all your heart to the standard of teaching in which you were instructed and to which you were committed. 18 And

having been set free from sin, you have become the slaves of righteousness [of conformity to God's will and purpose].

[19] I am speaking in [familiar] human terms because of your natural limitations [your spiritual immaturity]. For just as you presented your bodily members as slaves to impurity and to [moral] lawlessness, leading to further lawlessness, so now offer your members [your abilities, your talents] as slaves to righteousness, leading to [a]sanctification [that is, being set apart for God's purpose].

FOOTNOTES:

Romans 6:19 There are three basic kinds of sanctification in the NT: (1) Positional sanctification is based on the death of Christ. Every believer is a saint and is holy before God. The believer is "set apart for God" and in some instances "set apart for God's purpose" (Heb 10:10, 14, 29); (2) Practical sanctification is a progressive process and means "growing in righteous living" as the believer matures spiritually (Rom 6:13; 1 Thess 5:23; 1 Pet 1:16); (3) Ultimate sanctification is that which is to come when the believer stands before God (Eph 5:26, 27).

ROMANS 8:1-3 KING JAMES VERSION (KJV)

[1] There is therefore now no condemnation to them which are in Christ Jesus, who walk not after the flesh, but after the Spirit.

[2] For the law of the Spirit of life in Christ Jesus hath made me free from the law of sin and death.

[3] For what the law could not do, in that it was weak through the flesh, God sending his own Son in the likeness of sinful flesh, and for sin, condemned sin in the flesh:

Conclusion

His pardon costs us nothing but our willingness to be set free to experience a new way of living. He has paid all the fees needed to redeem us in the sacrifice of Christ Jesus. We cannot on our own accomplish that which He can do in us and for us. Therefore, He sends the Holy Spirit with an invitation and a magnifying glass which helps us to see where we stand in our walk without Him. We need to recognize that He can only do that which we are willing to accept. His pardon does have provisions but these provisions are for our freedom not continued imprisonment. We often hear it being said, "when I clean up my act then I will come to God." The problem is that we can't do enough to clean ourselves up to be acceptable to Him. There is a Christian song with the words "I will give my life tomorrow but tomorrow may well be too late." Many delay the call to repentance and miss the opportunities that are available. It is never too late to make a confession of repentance as long as it is genuine but scripture tells us that God will not always struggle with man. There is no limit to His to His patience. Our unwillingness is the only limitation. Only God can be the judge of that.

1 CORINTHIANS 6:9-11 AMPLIFIED BIBLE (AMP)

⁹ Do you not know that the unrighteous will not inherit or have any share in the kingdom of God? Do not be deceived; [d]neither the sexually immoral, nor idolaters, nor adulterers, nor effeminate [by perversion], nor [e]those who participate in homosexuality,

¹⁰ nor thieves, nor the greedy, nor drunkards, nor revilers [whose words are used as weapons to abuse, insult, humiliate, intimidate, or slander], nor swindlers will inherit or have any share in the kingdom of God.

¹¹ And such were some of you [before you believed]. But you were washed [by the atoning sacrifice of Christ], you were sanctified [set apart for God, and made holy], you were justified [declared free of guilt] in the name of the Lord Jesus Christ and in the [Holy] Spirit of our God [the source of the believer's new life and changed behavior].

FOOTNOTES:

1 Corinthians 6:9 This list of sinners, which continues into v 10, is used by Paul to describe various sinful lifestyles. All such lifestyles are impossible for true believers, who continue to sin but not to live lives of sin.

1 Corinthians 6:9 Lit male homosexuals.

The degree that we can experience this newfound freedom depends on our response to God's call for us to be open to the rejuvenation He can bring about in us as and the degree that we continue to be open to His leadings to do this. We have to learn a new way to express who we are and how we intend to use the newfound freedom He is providing. Nothing He does is done by force. It does require our cooperation and permission. Otherwise we are in a situation no different than we were before. It is a joint effort in that we need only be open to change and not resist the new-found way to live.

JAMES 5:19-20 AMPLIFIED BIBLE (AMP)

[19] My brothers and sisters, if anyone among you strays from the truth and falls into error and [another] one turns him back [to God], [20] let the [latter] one know that the one who has turned a sinner from the error of his way will save that one's soul from death and cover a multitude of sins [that is, obtain the pardon of the many sins committed by the one who has been restored].

1 JOHN 2:11-13 AMPLIFIED BIBLE (AMP)

[11] But the one who habitually hates (works against) his brother [in Christ] is in [spiritual] darkness and is walking in the darkness, and does not know where he is going because the darkness has blinded his eyes.

[12] I am writing to you, little children (believers, dear ones), because your sins have been forgiven for His name's sake [you have been pardoned and released from spiritual debt through His name because you have confessed His name, believing in Him as Savior].

[13] I am writing to you, fathers [those believers who are spiritually mature], because you know Him who has existed from the beginning. I am writing to you, young men [those believers who are growing in spiritual maturity], because you have been victorious and have overcome the evil one. I have written to you, children [those who are new believers, those spiritually immature], because you have come to know the Father.

CHAPTER 7

Right and Wrong

Is God portraying in scripture more of what is right and wrong through His commandments or through the cause and effect relationship in the choices we make? He states that each one of us has a conscience from which he is to be judged. He has created in each of us the inherent ability to sense when we are choosing what things are either right or wrong. Each choice we make either approves or disapproves, by way of our conscience, whether the choice is good or bad. Each choice is either excused or approved or disapproved by way of our conscience based on how we choose to make our choice. Yes, we have a choice to either agree with, or to compromise, or to ignore, or to negate what the conscience is telling us.

> **JOHN 8:31-32 KING JAMES VERSION (KJV)**
> **31 Then said Jesus to those Jews which believed on him, If ye continue in my word, then are ye my disciples indeed;**
> **32 And ye shall know the truth, and the truth shall make you free.**
> **ACTS 23:1 KING JAMES VERSION (KJV)**
> **1 And Paul, earnestly beholding the council, said, Men and brethren, I have lived in all good conscience before God until this day.**
> **ROMANS 9:1-2 KING JAMES VERSION (KJV)**
> **1 I say the truth in Christ, I lie not, my conscience also bearing me witness in the Holy Ghost,**
> **2 That I have great heaviness and continual sorrow in my heart.**

We excuse or approve our choices when we want to portray ourselves as self-righteous. God has built into us something that which acts as a gauge, which grades the choices we make. It is this built in device, which we call a conscience, that is placed within us to help us bring the light of right and wrong in our being.

JOHN 15:20-22 KING JAMES VERSION (KJV)

²⁰ Remember the word that I said unto you, The servant is not greater than his lord. If they have persecuted me, they will also persecute you; if they have kept my saying, they will keep yours also.

²¹ But all these things will they do unto you for my name's sake, because they know not him that sent me.

²² If I had not come and spoken unto them, they had not had sin: but now they have no cloak for their sin.

1 TIMOTHY 1:1-6 AMPLIFIED BIBLE (AMP)

Correcting False Teaching

¹ Paul, an apostle (special messenger, personally chosen representative) of Christ Jesus by the commandment of God our Savior, and of Christ Jesus (the Messiah, the Anointed) our Hope [the fulfillment of our salvation],

² to Timothy, my true son in the faith: Grace, mercy, and peace [inner calm and spiritual well-being] from God the Father and Christ Jesus our Lord.

³ As I urged you when I was on my way to Macedonia, stay on at Ephesus so that you may instruct certain individuals not to teach any different doctrines,

⁴ nor to pay attention to legends (fables, myths) and endless genealogies, which give rise to useless speculation and meaningless arguments rather than advancing God's program of instruction which is grounded in faith [and requires surrendering the entire self to God in absolute trust and confidence].

⁵ But the goal of our instruction is love [which springs] from a pure heart and a good conscience and a sincere faith.

⁶ Some individuals have wandered away from these things into empty arguments and useless discussions,

1 TIMOTHY 1:18-19 AMPLIFIED BIBLE (AMP)

¹⁸ This command I entrust to you, Timothy, my son, in accordance with the prophecies previously made concerning you, so that [inspired and aided] by them you may fight the good fight [in contending with false teachers],

¹⁹ keeping your faith [leaning completely on God with absolute trust and confidence in His guidance] and having a good conscience; for some [people] have rejected [their moral compass] and have made a shipwreck of their faith.

1 TIMOTHY 3:8-9 AMPLIFIED BIBLE (AMP)
8 [a]Deacons likewise must be men worthy of respect [honorable, financially ethical, of good character], not double-tongued [speakers of half-truths], not addicted to wine, not greedy for dishonest gain,
9 but upholding and fully understanding the mystery [that is, the true doctrine] of the [Christian] faith with a clear conscience [resulting from behavior consistent with spiritual maturity].

FOOTNOTES:
1 Timothy 3:8 Though the Greek word for "deacon" does not occur in Acts (only Paul uses it), it is generally thought that the origin of the office or ministry is found in Acts 6:1-6, where Luke reports that seven men were appointed to assist the church leaders in serving and ministering to members of the congregation.

ROMANS 2:1-19 AMPLIFIED BIBLE (AMP)
The Impartiality of God
1 Therefore you have no excuse or justification, everyone of you who [hypocritically] [a]judges and condemns others; for in passing judgment on another person, you condemn yourself, because you who judge [from a position of arrogance or self-righteousness] are habitually practicing the very same things [which you denounce].
2 And we know that the judgment of God falls justly and in accordance with truth on those who practice such things.
3 But do you think this, O man, when you judge and condemn those who practice such things, and yet do the same yourself, that you will escape God's judgment and elude His verdict?
4 Or do you have no regard for the wealth of His kindness and tolerance and patience [in withholding His wrath]? Are you [actually] unaware or ignorant [of the fact] that God's kindness leads you to repentance [that is, to change your inner self, your old way of thinking—seek His purpose for your life]?
5 But because of your callous stubbornness and unrepentant heart you are [deliberately] storing up wrath for yourself on the day of wrath when God's righteous judgment will be revealed.
6 He will pay back to each person according to his deeds [justly, as his deeds deserve]:
7 to those who by persistence in doing good seek [unseen but certain heavenly] glory, honor, and immortality, [He will give the gift of] eternal life.
8 But for those who are selfishly ambitious and self-seeking and disobedient to the truth but responsive to wickedness, [there will be] wrath and indignation.

[9] There will be tribulation and anguish [torturing confinement] for every human soul who does [or permits] evil, to the Jew first and also to the Greek,
[10] but glory and honor and inner peace [will be given] to everyone who habitually does good, to the Jew first and also to the Greek.
[11] For God shows no partiality [no arbitrary favoritism; with Him one person is not more important than another].
[12] For all who have sinned without the Law will also perish without [regard to] the Law, and all who have sinned under the Law will be judged and condemned by the Law.
[13] For it is not those who merely hear the Law [as it is read aloud] who are just or righteous before God, but it is those who [actually] obey the Law who will be [b]justified [pronounced free of the guilt of sin and declared acceptable to Him].
[14] When Gentiles, who do not have the Law [since it was given only to Jews], do [c]instinctively the things the Law requires [guided only by their conscience], they are a law to themselves, though they do not have the Law.
[15] They show that the [d]essential requirements of the Law are written in their hearts; and their conscience [their sense of right and wrong, their moral choices] bearing witness and their thoughts alternately accusing or perhaps defending them
[16] on that day when, [e]as my gospel proclaims, God will judge the secrets [all the hidden thoughts and concealed sins] of men through Christ Jesus.
The Jew Is Condemned by the Law
[17] But if you bear the name "Jew" and rely on the Law [for your salvation] and boast in [your special relationship to] God,
[18] and [if you claim to] know His will and [f]approve the things that are [g]essential or have a sense of what is excellent, based on your instruction from the Law,
[19] and [if you] are confident that you are a [qualified] guide to the blind [those untaught in theology], a light to those who are in darkness,

FOOTNOTES:

Romans 2:1 This is not a prohibition of judgment, nor is it a command to stop using godly wisdom, common sense, and moral courage together with God's written word to discern right from wrong, to distinguish between morality and immorality, and to judge doctrinal truth. There are many judgments that are not only legitimate, but are commanded (cf John 7:24; 1 Cor 5:5, 12; Gal 1:8,

9; 1 John 4:1-3; 2 John 10); however, you cannot judge another if
you are committing the same type of sin.
Romans 2:13 Because of one's personal faith in Jesus Christ as
Savior, God graciously credits His righteousness to the believer.
Justification denotes a legal standing with God as designated only
by God. God declares a believer to be acquitted or innocent, then
designates the believer to be brought into right standing before
Him.
Romans 2:14 Lit by nature.
Romans 2:15 Lit work of the Law.
Romans 2:16 Lit according to my gospel.
Romans 2:18 Or discerningly distinguish between the things which
differ.
Romans 2:18 Or excellent.

The way our conscience works is sort of like judging whether the tire pressure in our car is in the right range. The car and tire makers recommend the correct pressure required for a particular tire. We choose to inflate it either above or below the recommended level or choose to ignore it completely. If we choose to operate the tire with a pressure that is too low or too high, we decrease the life of the tire and its effectiveness or we can even destroy it. The manufacturers warn that operating outside the recommended range can be dangerous because we are operating outside of the design limits for which the tire was created. Therefore, if we want to operate the tire within the limits for which it was created, we follow the prescribed rules. If not, we suffer the consequences. Here we see a cause and effect relationship, much the same as how our conscience works.

We can wear out or destroy the built-in choice of right and wrong in ourselves. We either become more hardened toward the operation of this built-in system or we become more sensitive to its presence. Therefore, we either decide to allow it to continue to operate or we dismiss its use entirely or somewhere in between. Just as stated in above in Romans 2, the conscience, our thoughts from our spirit are in constant communication regarding our choices. Our conscience has the prescribed instruction in it. All we need to do is follow it. Let's see something about this in scripture.

GENESIS 20:1-6 AMPLIFIED BIBLE (AMP)
Abraham's Deception

[1] *Now Abraham journeyed from there toward the Negev (the South country), and settled between Kadesh and Shur; then he lived temporarily in Gerar.*

[2] *Abraham [a]said [again] of Sarah his wife, "She is my sister." So [b]Abimelech king of Gerar sent and took [c]Sarah [into his harem].*

[3] *But God came to Abimelech in a dream during the night, and said, "Behold, you are a dead man because of the woman whom you have taken [as your wife], for she is another man's wife."*

[4] *Now Abimelech had not yet come near her; so he said, "Lord, will you kill a people who are righteous and innocent and blameless [regarding Sarah]?* [5] *Did Abraham not tell me, 'She is my sister?' And she herself said, 'He is my brother.' In the integrity of my heart and innocence of my hands I have done this."*

[6] *Then God said to him in the dream, "Yes, I know you did this in the integrity of your heart, for it was I who kept you back and spared you from sinning against Me; therefore I did not give you an opportunity to touch her.*

FOOTNOTES:

Genesis 20:2 See 12:11-13.

Genesis 20:2 The word "Abimelech" may be a royal title instead of a proper name. In either case this man is probably the father or grandfather of Abimelech king of the Philistines encountered later by Isaac (26:1).

Genesis 20:2 Sarah was about ninety years old at this time.

1 TIMOTHY 4:1-3 KING JAMES VERSION (KJV)

[1] *Now the Spirit speaketh expressly, that in the latter times some shall depart from the faith, giving heed to seducing spirits, and doctrines of devils;*

[2] *Speaking lies in hypocrisy; having their conscience seared with a hot iron;*

[3] *Forbidding to marry, and commanding to abstain from meats, which God hath created to be received with thanksgiving of them which believe and know the truth.*

In Genesis chapter 20 above, it was the conscience of the king, not Abraham or his wife that was kicked into action that prevented Abraham's wife from being taken into adultery. It was the king's admission of adultery being wrong which shows his conscience was working. Note that the chosen of God had lied and it was the king who responded to the built-in mechanism of right and wrong within himself. It was this which caused him to confront Abraham and his wife about the lie they were perpetrating. See also how Abraham and his wife had consoled their conscience by twisting their reasoning in stating what they did was OK because they were genuinely brother and sister. They were consoling their own conscience (twisting it through justifying a wrong by hiding a lie in the truth). Haven't most of us done the same? I know I have many times.

Just about every gadget in modern society has a set of instructions provided. The instructions are provided so that we can properly achieve the maker's design and gadget's intended purpose. I can relate to this because many times when I had brought a new toy which required assembly for my kids, I chose to not use the instructions. I would choose to use my limited knowledge and ignore the instructions. I would wing it and do it my way and guess the way to go about assembling the toy. More often than not, I would end up finding out that I had left out a step and the dang thing would not work as intended and some pieces did not seem to fit together and other parts were left lying on the ground. These pieces were to be installed but I had no clue as to where or how. Then I figured out I needed to read the instructions. You would think I would have figured out after the first time that it was important to read the instructions first but I didn't do it. So, I kept repeating the same errors over and over. There was, most of the time the nagging little voice inside of me saying "read the instructions first." Now I have learned my lesson so now I read the instructions first and then I search on line for a video depicting the installation. I have found that these steps have helped prevent many mistakes.

Our consciences are similar to this. They are like a limit switch to help us choose the right way to go about living our lives. They send a warning signal when we are about to go outside the limits which are good for us and others. Many don't understand that our conscience has been deliberately provided for this purpose and are not aware of why it exists. It's similar to the automatic systems placed in our bodies. Like the circulatory system or the respiratory or digestive systems that operate without our direction or input. These systems were designed to keep our bodies working as intended. Even though they operate without us thinking through what they are required to do, they determine the ability of our body to function properly. Yet, we can by choice of life style either improve the operation of these systems or we can impair them. Our conscience is the same way. It can operate as designed or it can be impaired by our choosing to reason our way around it. Scripture puts it this way we reason based on what the conscience dictates or we can come up with reasons to work around the guidance of the conscience. Refer to Romans 2 above. Our intelligence many times can be either an aid or an enemy to our conscience since we can justify our actions through our mind.

> **2 TIMOTHY 1:1-3 KING JAMES VERSION (KJV)**
> *¹ Paul, an apostle of Jesus Christ by the will of God, according to the promise of life which is in Christ Jesus,*
> *² To Timothy, my dearly beloved son: Grace, mercy, and peace, from God the Father and Christ Jesus our Lord.*
> *³ I thank God, whom I serve from my forefathers with pure conscience, that without ceasing I have remembrance of thee in my prayers night and day;*

Speaking of guidance let's look at an automated guidance system as is used in aircraft. That device has been preprogrammed to do things a certain way so that an aircraft stays on course. A pilot can use this device to aid him on staying on course or he can ignore it or even shut it off. In much the same way the conscience is preprogrammed to guide us into making choices to stay on course. As stated before, we can use it or ignore it or turn it around to suit our desires or shut it off.

I believe from this we can all say that we have a conscience or have had one at one time in our lives. It has been provided as a guidance system for our lives. The instructions in it can be used to help us make the right choices or we can abuse it by reorienting its preprogrammed instruction to fit what our viewpoint of life is.

So now we get into what is right and what is wrong. Things which are consistent with the preprogrammed instruction set in our conscience is right and that which goes against it or is modified by us is wrong. The conscience works against the other built-in part of us which is the inbuilt desire we have to put ourselves first and our lustful desires. So, the conscience and our desires can either be used in support of each other or we can allow one or the other to dominate the choices we make in life. They both are built in us to provide us the with the ability to have free will to choose who or what we will follow.

There are three spirits in this world: the spirit of man, the Holy Spirit and the spirit of the evil one. We are influenced by each of these in conjunction with the workings of our conscience. The programming of our conscience is designed to work in compliance with the works of the Holy Spirit because it is God that has provided the programming of our conscience to coincide with His good works but either of these spirits can affect how the conscience works. Each of us has this mechanism built into us. Yet, many don't recognize that it is there. Just as many deny the existence of God, many don't allow the conscience to perform as it was originally intended. So, we follow one of the two sprits, mainly that of our inner will (the spirit of man) or the spirit of the evil one, or both in some degree or the other, and subvert the work of the conscience and leave it in a realm of uselessness. When this happens, we start drifting away from the true intent for which the conscience exists and sin is our goal, rather than the righteousness of God.

HEBREWS 9:11-15 KING JAMES VERSION (KJV)

11 But Christ being come an high priest of good things to come, by a greater and more perfect tabernacle, not made with hands, that is to say, not of this building;

12 Neither by the blood of goats and calves, but by his own blood he entered in once into the holy place, having obtained eternal redemption for us.

13 For if the blood of bulls and of goats, and the ashes of an heifer sprinkling the unclean, sanctifieth to the purifying of the flesh:

14 How much more shall the blood of Christ, who through the eternal Spirit offered himself without spot to God, purge your conscience from dead works to serve the living God?

15 And for this cause he is the mediator of the new testament, that by means of death, for the redemption of the transgressions that were under the first testament, they which are called might receive the promise of eternal inheritance.

HEBREWS 10:16-23 KING JAMES VERSION (KJV)

16 This is the covenant that I will make with them after those days, saith the Lord, I will put my laws into their hearts, and in their minds will I write them;

17 And their sins and iniquities will I remember no more.

18 Now where remission of these is, there is no more offering for sin.

19 Having therefore, brethren, boldness to enter into the holiest by the blood of Jesus,

20 By a new and living way, which he hath consecrated for us, through the veil, that is to say, his flesh;

21 And having an high priest over the house of God;

²² Let us draw near with a true heart in full assurance of faith, having our hearts sprinkled from an evil conscience, and our bodies washed with pure water.
²³ Let us hold fast the profession of our faith without wavering; (for he is faithful that promised;)

Conclusion

The conscience is designed to help us develop the right relationship to all that is around us: the creation, our fellow man and first and most of all, God. If we recognize this, then the conscience becomes a mighty force in establishing who we are and what we are to become. If we do not follow its leadings, we can develop a sense of hopelessness or a sense of being lost or a sense of confusion in our lives. So many have succumbed to the subtle yet disruptive sides of our personalities and with the help of the evil one we stray far from the usefulness that the conscience was designed to provide in our lives.

God has equipped us all with the sense of what is right and wrong through the work of the conscience. So, it is this medium which can help us stay on track with our existence and the existence of that that which is around us, all His creation. We become off balance without it. Some are able to make the adjustment that keeps our equilibrium or balance even though it is not as it is intended. Others get so conflicted within themselves that life becomes overwhelming and they are at a loss to see the value in their existence. This is the goal of the evil one to promote the sense of loss and uselessness in our existence so that we cannot perceive the creator and His good will for us all and the need for relationship with Him or the fact that He even exists. Yes, it is this useless feeling that leads many to commit suicide or causes many to become depressed. As scripture states the devil comes to kill steal and destroy.

1 CORINTHIANS 14:31-33 KING JAMES VERSION (KJV)
³¹ For ye may all prophesy one by one, that all may learn, and all may be comforted.
³² And the spirits of the prophets are subject to the prophets.
³³ For God is not the author of confusion, but of peace, as in all churches of the saints.

Yes, there is an internal conflict that exists within each of us. The two parts of us which work against or in cooperation with each other (the will to do right and the will to go against the built-in standard of right and wrong within us). Herein lies our free will. There is a constant battle or struggle which we many times don't recognize. Many have learned to bypass this or even ignore this. Some have even learned to turn it off so they can pursue a life of self-indulgence far from the leadings of the work of the conscience. They then provide an open door to the workings of the evil one. The devil's goal is to destroy the work of the conscience which was placed in us to bring us into the life for which we were created. The devil can then attempt to bring about the destruction of our souls and increase the separation between us and God.

JAMES 1:19-24 KING JAMES VERSION (KJV)

[19] Wherefore, my beloved brethren, let every man be swift to hear, slow to speak, slow to wrath:

[20] For the wrath of man worketh not the righteousness of God.

[21] Wherefore lay apart all filthiness and superfluity of naughtiness, and receive with meekness the engrafted word, which is able to save your souls.

[22] But be ye doers of the word, and not hearers only, deceiving your own selves.

[23] For if any be a hearer of the word, and not a doer, he is like unto a man beholding his natural face in a glass:

[24] For he beholdeth himself, and goeth his way, and straightway forgetteth what manner of man he was.

JAMES 3:13-18 KING JAMES VERSION (KJV)

[13] Who is a wise man and endued with knowledge among you? let him shew out of a good conversation his works with meekness of wisdom.

[14] But if ye have bitter envying and strife in your hearts, glory not, and lie not against the truth.

[15] This wisdom descendeth not from above, but is earthly, sensual, devilish.

[16] For where envying and strife is, there is confusion and every evil work.

[17] But the wisdom that is from above is first pure, then peaceable, gentle, and easy to be intreated, full of mercy and good fruits, without partiality, and without hypocrisy.

18 And the fruit of righteousness is sown in peace of them that make peace.

PSALM 60:1-5 KING JAMES VERSION (KJV)

1 O God, thou hast cast us off, thou hast scattered us, thou hast been displeased; O turn thyself to us again.

2 Thou hast made the earth to tremble; thou hast broken it: heal the breaches thereof; for it shaketh.

3 Thou hast shewed thy people hard things: thou hast made us to drink the wine of astonishment.

4 Thou hast given a banner to them that fear thee, that it may be displayed because of the truth. Selah.

5 That thy beloved may be delivered; save with thy right hand, and hear me.

The instruction and commandments in scripture provide a source to rejuvenate the conscience and reinforce its programming so that it can work as intended and bring us into the right relationship with ourselves, others and God. As stated, before the work of the scripture has to be influenced by the power of the Holy Spirit. An example is the Ethiopian who needed Phillip to come to his rescue and guide him into understanding the meaning of the words which make up scripture. It is not that we are illiterate but that our understanding has been darkened by the choice to invoke our power to disrupt the work of the conscience which relates to the prompting of the Holy Spirit.

That is why I have been led by the Spirit to read scripture. He has many times provided within me an insatiable desire to read and understand scripture. It is sometimes so overwhelming that I can't rest until I fulfill the point God wants me to understand and gain through the guidance in scripture. I offer thanks to one our ministers who through his commitment to his calling introduced me to the workings of the Holy Spirit in my work as one of God's servants.

You know as I was about to start this chapter, I did not have an understanding of what to say or to where it was to lead us and I did not have a clear picture of its intent. As scripture states, sometimes we see through a glass darkly not being able to ascertain the light. I, just as some of you, am not yet perfect. God has blessed me to write this work. I still have a long way to go on the road to perfection and being remade into the image God created me to be. Though I may not at this moment be able to emulate Christ Jesus, I have had many experiences which indicate that He is preparing me for this leap into the calling we all can achieve.

When I stepped out in faith and just started writing the words started flowing and the content jumped on the pages. It was through the work of the Spirit and not my intelligence these words came.

Many are called but few are chosen. The opportunity exists for each of us but our response and willingness to heed this call makes the difference. I am not much different from most of you. I too have sinned in so many ways, yet as King David, I heed the call of the Spirit to most of the time repent. Now don't say I am comparing myself to King David. I can only identify with how the Spirit has worked in both of us.

1 PETER 3:18-22 KING JAMES VERSION (KJV)
18 For Christ also hath once suffered for sins, the just for the unjust, that he might bring us to God, being put to death in the flesh, but quickened by the Spirit:
19 By which also he went and preached unto the spirits in prison;
20 Which sometime were disobedient, when once the longsuffering of God waited in the days of Noah, while the ark was a preparing, wherein few, that is, eight souls were saved by water.
21 The like figure whereunto even baptism doth also now save us (not the putting away of the filth of the flesh, but the answer of a good conscience toward God,) by the resurrection of Jesus Christ:
22 Who is gone into heaven, and is on the right hand of God; angels and authorities and powers being made subject unto him.

Yes, the words He spoke to me so many years ago when I was choosing to leave this church after becoming discouraged with some of the people in it (If you were baptized into a church. Then there was a period of silence, then He continued on, but If you were baptized unto me you are in this for eternity) still resonate within my being. I provide the full testimony of this in my first book. Now, I am looking forward to spending the rest of my eternal existence in His presence. Some question my claim to have heard Him. Others have no question about this. Where do you stand and are you listening for His voice? Remember how scripture describes the voice of God calling out to a young man by name, Samuel:

1 SAMUEL 3:1-10 KING JAMES VERSION (KJV)
3 And the child Samuel ministered unto the Lord before Eli. And the word of the Lord was precious in those days; there was no open vision.

² And it came to pass at that time, when Eli was laid down in his place, and his eyes began to wax dim, that he could not see;

³ And ere the lamp of God went out in the temple of the Lord, where the ark of God was, and Samuel was laid down to sleep;

⁴ That the Lord called Samuel: and he answered, Here am I.

⁵ And he ran unto Eli, and said, Here am I; for thou calledst me. And he said, I called not; lie down again. And he went and lay down.

⁶ And the Lord called yet again, Samuel. And Samuel arose and went to Eli, and said, Here am I; for thou didst call me. And he answered, I called not, my son; lie down again.

⁷ Now Samuel did not yet know the Lord, neither was the word of the Lord yet revealed unto him.

⁸ And the Lord called Samuel again the third time. And he arose and went to Eli, and said, Here am I; for thou didst call me. And Eli perceived that the Lord had called the child.

⁹ Therefore Eli said unto Samuel, Go, lie down: and it shall be, if he call thee, that thou shalt say, Speak, Lord; for thy servant heareth. So Samuel went and lay down in his place.

¹⁰ And the Lord came, and stood, and called as at other times, Samuel, Samuel. Then Samuel answered, Speak; for thy servant heareth.

2 CORINTHIANS 4:1-8 KING JAMES VERSION (KJV)

⁴ Therefore seeing we have this ministry, as we have received mercy, we faint not;

² But have renounced the hidden things of dishonesty, not walking in craftiness, nor handling the word of God deceitfully; but by manifestation of the truth commending ourselves to every man's conscience in the sight of God.

³ But if our gospel be hid, it is hid to them that are lost:

⁴ In whom the god of this world hath blinded the minds of them which believe not, lest the light of the glorious gospel of Christ, who is the image of God, should shine unto them.

⁵ For we preach not ourselves, but Christ Jesus the Lord; and ourselves your servants for Jesus' sake.

⁶ For God, who commanded the light to shine out of darkness, hath shined in our hearts, to give the light of the knowledge of the glory of God in the face of Jesus Christ.

⁷ But we have this treasure in earthen vessels, that the excellency of the power may be of God, and not of us.

⁸ We are troubled on every side, yet not distressed; we are perplexed, but not in despair;

MATTHEW 22:1-14 KING JAMES VERSION (KJV)

1 And Jesus answered and spake unto them again by parables, and said,

2 The kingdom of heaven is like unto a certain king, which made a marriage for his son,

3 And sent forth his servants to call them that were bidden to the wedding: and they would not come.

4 Again, he sent forth other servants, saying, Tell them which are bidden, Behold, I have prepared my dinner: my oxen and my fatlings are killed, and all things are ready: come unto the marriage.

5 But they made light of it, and went their ways, one to his farm, another to his merchandise:

6 And the remnant took his servants, and entreated them spitefully, and slew them.

7 But when the king heard thereof, he was wroth: and he sent forth his armies, and destroyed those murderers, and burned up their city.

8 Then saith he to his servants, The wedding is ready, but they which were bidden were not worthy.

9 Go ye therefore into the highways, and as many as ye shall find, bid to the marriage.

10 So those servants went out into the highways, and gathered together all as many as they found, both bad and good: and the wedding was furnished with guests.

11 And when the king came in to see the guests, he saw there a man which had not on a wedding garment:

12 And he saith unto him, Friend, how camest thou in hither not having a wedding garment? And he was speechless.

13 Then said the king to the servants, Bind him hand and foot, and take him away, and cast him into outer darkness, there shall be weeping and gnashing of teeth.

14 For many are called, but few are chosen.

The devil understands how the conscience works. He knows he can entice us with our selfish desires to subvert it just as he tried to do when he tried to get Jesus to misconstrue scripture for His fame and fortune in the desert encounter. The devil also knows that he can use the conscience to bear guilt on us. He knows the purpose of the conscience and tries to turn it against us. We have been redeemed by the blood of the Lamb (Jesus the Christ) and if we have properly followed the steps of repentance, by faith we know that there is no condemnation to us who follow Christ Jesus.

CHAPTER 8

Repentance

Repentance is a response to the call from the Holy Spirit to recognize God is seeking to restore us to righteousness. First it is a move made by God Himself on our behalf to restore us to the place He intended for us before we even recognized Him as Creator. There is statement in scripture where God wants us to see how highly He regards man. Here He states we were created just a little lower than the angels.

PSALM 8:1-9 KING JAMES VERSION (KJV)
¹ O Lord, our Lord, how excellent is thy name in all the earth! who hast set thy glory above the heavens.
² Out of the mouth of babes and sucklings hast thou ordained strength because of thine enemies, that thou mightest still the enemy and the avenger.
³ When I consider thy heavens, the work of thy fingers, the moon and the stars, which thou hast ordained;
⁴ What is man, that thou art mindful of him? and the son of man, that thou visitest him?
⁵ For thou hast made him a little lower than the angels, and hast crowned him with glory and honour.
⁶ Thou madest him to have dominion over the works of thy hands; thou hast put all things under his feet:
⁷ All sheep and oxen, yea, and the beasts of the field;
⁸ The fowl of the air, and the fish of the sea, and whatsoever passeth through the paths of the seas.
⁹ O Lord our Lord, how excellent is thy name in all the earth!
HEBREWS 2:1-13 KING JAMES VERSION (KJV)
¹ Therefore we ought to give the more earnest heed to the things which we have heard, lest at any time we should let them slip.

² For if the word spoken by angels was stedfast, and every transgression and disobedience received a just recompence of reward;
³ How shall we escape, if we neglect so great salvation; which at the first began to be spoken by the Lord, and was confirmed unto us by them that heard him;
⁴ God also bearing them witness, both with signs and wonders, and with divers miracles, and gifts of the Holy Ghost, according to his own will?
⁵ For unto the angels hath he not put in subjection the world to come, whereof we speak.
⁶ But one in a certain place testified, saying, What is man, that thou art mindful of him? or the son of man that thou visitest him?
⁷ Thou madest him a little lower than the angels; thou crownedst him with glory and honour, and didst set him over the works of thy hands:
⁸ Thou hast put all things in subjection under his feet. For in that he put all in subjection under him, he left nothing that is not put under him. But now we see not yet all things put under him.
⁹ But we see Jesus, who was made a little lower than the angels for the suffering of death, crowned with glory and honour; that he by the grace of God should taste death for every man.
¹⁰ For it became him, for whom are all things, and by whom are all things, in bringing many sons unto glory, to make the captain of their salvation perfect through sufferings.
¹¹ For both he that sanctifieth and they who are sanctified are all of one: for which cause he is not ashamed to call them brethren,
¹² Saying, I will declare thy name unto my brethren, in the midst of the church will I sing praise unto thee.
¹³ And again, I will put my trust in him. And again, Behold I and the children which God hath given me.

In Psalm 8 and also Hebrews 2 we have a glimpse of how highly God regards man. Wow! Is it not a privilege to be set on such a high pedestal? Not only does it state God's purpose in creating us it also provides insight into His ultimate will for us. Note verse 2 in Psalm 8 where it is stated that He intends to silence the enemy and the avenger. Do you understand this statement? Do you know who the enemy of God is and who is the avenger? Let's look into this first as we consider the work of repentance.

Who or what is it that God can have as an enemy? Who or what is it that can be at war with the most powerful one in creation, He who made the entire creation and at the end of the description of each step declared it as good? How then can any part of something that He himself made be His enemy? When you consider how carefully God made all things and the fact that each part of His creation has a specific use, then how can it be an enemy? Well consider this. Out of His love for us He made in us, His creation, the ability to choose to use Him and His ways as our example. When we choose not to follow Him and His ways and turn against Him, we are an enemy to Him. Yes, when we exercise our choice to go against His righteousness, we choose sin rather than Him and separate ourselves from His grace and love. In one term, simply put, it is sin in our lives (our carnal mind) which makes us the enemy. The sin in our lives or sin in any part of His creation is His enemy. Scripture tells us God cannot tolerate sin in the least bit and He will not allow it in His presence.

GENESIS 3:15:1 KING JAMES VERSION (KJV)

1 And I will put enmity between thee and the woman, and between thy seed and her seed; it shall bruise thy head, and thou shalt bruise his heel.

ROMANS 8:1-11 KING JAMES VERSION (KJV)

1 There is therefore now no condemnation to them which are in Christ Jesus, who walk not after the flesh, but after the Spirit.

2 For the law of the Spirit of life in Christ Jesus hath made me free from the law of sin and death.

3 For what the law could not do, in that it was weak through the flesh, God sending his own Son in the likeness of sinful flesh, and for sin, condemned sin in the flesh:

4 That the righteousness of the law might be fulfilled in us, who walk not after the flesh, but after the Spirit.

5 For they that are after the flesh do mind the things of the flesh; but they that are after the Spirit the things of the Spirit.

6 For to be carnally minded is death; but to be spiritually minded is life and peace.

7 Because the carnal mind is enmity against God: for it is not subject to the law of God, neither indeed can be.

8 So then they that are in the flesh cannot please God.

9 But ye are not in the flesh, but in the Spirit, if so be that the Spirit of God dwell in you. Now if any man have not the Spirit of Christ, he is none of his.

10 And if Christ be in you, the body is dead because of sin; but the Spirit is life because of righteousness.

11 But if the Spirit of him that raised up Jesus from the dead dwell in you, he that raised up Christ from the dead shall also quicken your mortal bodies by his Spirit that dwelleth in you.

JAMES 4:1-7 KING JAMES VERSION (KJV)

1 From whence come wars and fightings among you? come they not hence, even of your lusts that war in your members?

2 Ye lust, and have not: ye kill, and desire to have, and cannot obtain: ye fight and war, yet ye have not, because ye ask not.

3 Ye ask, and receive not, because ye ask amiss, that ye may consume it upon your lusts.

4 Ye adulterers and adulteresses, know ye not that the friendship of the world is enmity with God? whosoever therefore will be a friend of the world is the enemy of God.

5 Do ye think that the scripture saith in vain, The spirit that dwelleth In us lusteth to envy?

6 But he giveth more grace. Wherefore he saith, God resisteth the proud, but giveth grace unto the humble.

7 Submit yourselves therefore to God. Resist the devil, and he will flee from you.

PROVERBS 3:19-32 KING JAMES VERSION (KJV)

19 The Lord by wisdom hath founded the earth; by understanding hath he established the heavens.

20 By his knowledge the depths are broken up, and the clouds drop down the dew.

21 My son, let not them depart from thine eyes: keep sound wisdom and discretion:

22 So shall they be life unto thy soul, and grace to thy neck.

23 Then shalt thou walk in thy way safely, and thy foot shall not stumble.

24 When thou liest down, thou shalt not be afraid: yea, thou shalt lie down, and thy sleep shall be sweet.

25 Be not afraid of sudden fear, neither of the desolation of the wicked, when it cometh.

26 For the Lord shall be thy confidence, and shall keep thy foot from being taken.

27 Withhold not good from them to whom it is due, when it is in the power of thine hand to do it.

28 Say not unto thy neighbour, Go, and come again, and to morrow I will give; when thou hast it by thee.

29 Devise not evil against thy neighbour, seeing he dwelleth securely by thee.

[30] Strive not with a man without cause, if he have done thee no harm.

[31] Envy thou not the oppressor, and choose none of his ways.

[32] For the froward is abomination to the Lord: but his secret is with the righteous.

PROVERBS 6:16-35 KING JAMES VERSION (KJV)

[16] These six things doth the Lord hate: yea, seven are an abomination unto him:

[17] A proud look, a lying tongue, and hands that shed innocent blood,

[18] An heart that deviseth wicked imaginations, feet that be swift in running to mischief,

[19] A false witness that speaketh lies, and he that soweth discord among brethren.

[20] My son, keep thy father's commandment, and forsake not the law of thy mother:

[21] Bind them continually upon thine heart, and tie them about thy neck.

[22] When thou goest, it shall lead thee; when thou sleepest, it shall keep thee; and when thou awakest, it shall talk with thee.

[23] For the commandment is a lamp; and the law is light; and reproofs of instruction are the way of life:

[24] To keep thee from the evil woman, from the flattery of the tongue of a strange woman.

[25] Lust not after her beauty in thine heart; neither let her take thee with her eyelids.

[26] For by means of a whorish woman a man is brought to a piece of bread: and the adultress will hunt for the precious life.

[27] Can a man take fire in his bosom, and his clothes not be burned?

[28] Can one go upon hot coals, and his feet not be burned?

[29] So he that goeth in to his neighbour's wife; whosoever toucheth her shall not be innocent.

[30] Men do not despise a thief, if he steal to satisfy his soul when he is hungry;

[31] But if he be found, he shall restore sevenfold; he shall give all the substance of his house.

[32] But whoso committeth adultery with a woman lacketh understanding: he that doeth it destroyeth his own soul.

[33] A wound and dishonour shall he get; and his reproach shall not be wiped away.

[34] For jealousy is the rage of a man: therefore he will not spare in the day of vengeance.

³⁵ He will not regard any ransom; neither will he rest content, though thou givest many gifts.

Conclusion

God fights against His enemy with love. It's not the way man wars against his foe. It is the love of God that seeks to redeem us and not let us be lost. As scripture states God roams the earth seeking to save those who are willing to heed His invitation to repentance. True repentance is for us to give up envying and lusting and submit to the work of the Holy Spirit which will teach us the ways of God. We have to humble ourselves admitting that God is the one and only true God and that the way we have lived is wrong and we need His righteousness imbedded in us for we are unable to do this ourselves. We have become like a computer with a virus (sin) and only the One who has the right tools and knowledge can fix it.

JOHN 4:22-24 KING JAMES VERSION (KJV)
²² Ye worship ye know not what: we know what we worship: for salvation is of the Jews.
²³ But the hour cometh, and now is, when the true worshippers shall worship the Father in spirit and in truth: for the Father seeketh such to worship him.
²⁴ God is a Spirit: and they that worship him must worship him in spirit and in truth.

EZEKIEL 34:9-16 KING JAMES VERSION (KJV)
⁹ Therefore, O ye shepherds, hear the word of the Lord;
¹⁰ Thus saith the Lord God; Behold, I am against the shepherds; and I will require my flock at their hand, and cause them to cease from feeding the flock; neither shall the shepherds feed themselves any more; for I will deliver my flock from their mouth, that they may not be meat for them.
¹¹ For thus saith the Lord God; Behold, I, even I, will both search my sheep, and seek them out.
¹² As a shepherd seeketh out his flock in the day that he is among his sheep that are scattered; so will I seek out my sheep, and will deliver them out of all places where they have been scattered in the cloudy and dark day.
¹³ And I will bring them out from the people, and gather them from the countries, and will bring them to their own land, and feed them

upon the mountains of Israel by the rivers, and in all the inhabited places of the country.

14 I will feed them in a good pasture, and upon the high mountains of Israel shall their fold be: there shall they lie in a good fold, and in a fat pasture shall they feed upon the mountains of Israel.

15 I will feed my flock, and I will cause them to lie down, saith the Lord God.

16 I will seek that which was lost, and bring again that which was driven away, and will bind up that which was broken, and will strengthen that which was sick: but I will destroy the fat and the strong;

CHAPTER 9

Return Love for Love

Does the bible teach that we should only love those who love us? I don't think so, but it does teach us to love as God loves, for He first loved us. This is one of the most overlooked parts of the gospel. We try to avoid this whenever possible. Yet God states that all things should have as its foundation love. Jesus made this famous statement that is quoted quite frequently, yet it is not lived out in the lives of most Christians. Jesus stated (paraphrasing what He said) that we should love the Lord our God with all our heart and mind and strength and to love our neighbors as ourselves. In this, He stated every commandment and all that we are called upon to do and be is embodied in the act of love. Do you know he was just quoting what was written in the Old Testament?

LEVITICUS 19:33-35 KING JAMES VERSION (KJV)
33 And if a stranger sojourn with thee in your land, ye shall not vex him.
34 But the stranger that dwelleth with you shall be unto you as one born among you, and thou shalt love him as thyself; for ye were strangers in the land of Egypt: I am the Lord your God.
35 Ye shall do no unrighteousness in judgment, in meteyard, in weight, or in measure.
DEUTERONOMY 6:4-6 KING JAMES VERSION (KJV)
4 Hear, O Israel: The Lord our God is one Lord:
5 And thou shalt love the Lord thy God with all thine heart, and with all thy soul, and with all thy might.
6 And these words, which I command thee this day, shall be in thine heart:

DEUTERONOMY 10:11-13 KING JAMES VERSION (KJV)

[11] *And the Lord said unto me, Arise, take thy journey before the people, that they may go in and possess the land, which I sware unto their fathers to give unto them.*

[12] *And now, Israel, what doth the Lord thy God require of thee, but to fear the Lord thy God, to walk in all his ways, and to love him, and to serve the Lord thy God with all thy heart and with all thy soul,*

[13] *To keep the commandments of the Lord, and his statutes, which I command thee this day for thy good?*

MATTHEW 22:36-38 KING JAMES VERSION (KJV)

[36] *Master, which is the great commandment in the law?*

[37] *Jesus said unto him, Thou shalt love the Lord thy God with all thy heart, and with all thy soul, and with all thy mind.*

[38] *This is the first and great commandment.*

MARK 12:29-31 KING JAMES VERSION (KJV)

[29] *And Jesus answered him, The first of all the commandments is, Hear, O Israel; The Lord our God is one Lord:*

[30] *And thou shalt love the Lord thy God with all thy heart, and with all thy soul, and with all thy mind, and with all thy strength: this is the first commandment.*

[31] *And the second is like, namely this, Thou shalt love thy neighbour as thyself. There is none other commandment greater than these.*

LUKE 10:23-28 KING JAMES VERSION (KJV)

[23] *And he turned him unto his disciples, and said privately, Blessed are the eyes which see the things that ye see:*

[24] *For I tell you, that many prophets and kings have desired to see those things which ye see, and have not seen them; and to hear those things which ye hear, and have not heard them.*

[25] *And, behold, a certain lawyer stood up, and tempted him, saying, Master, what shall I do to inherit eternal life?*

[26] *He said unto him, What is written in the law? how readest thou?*

[27] *And he answering said, Thou shalt love the Lord thy God with all thy heart, and with all thy soul, and with all thy strength, and with all thy mind; and thy neighbour as thyself.*

[28] *And he said unto him, Thou hast answered right: this do, and thou shalt live.*

LUKE 7:46-48 KING JAMES VERSION (KJV)

[46] *My head with oil thou didst not anoint: but this woman hath anointed my feet with ointment.*

⁴⁷ Wherefore I say unto thee, Her sins, which are many, are forgiven; for she loved much: but to whom little is forgiven, the same loveth little.

⁴⁸ And he said unto her, Thy sins are forgiven.

Yet, He also stated that we should hate sin. Here is a paradox - love and hate. How is this possible? How can we love everyone and not hate the sinner? How can we separate love for the sinner and hate the sins committed? Let's look into this aspect of the gospel. Before I continue with this, I am going to point this out in the scripture so no one can say, "Where did you get this from."

LEVITICUS 19:16-18 AMPLIFIED BIBLE (AMP)

¹⁶ You shall not go around as a gossip among your people, and you are not to act against the life of your neighbor [with slander or false testimony]; I am the Lord.

¹⁷ 'You shall not hate your brother in your heart; you may most certainly rebuke your neighbor, but shall not incur sin because of him.

¹⁸ You shall not take revenge nor bear any grudge against the sons of your people, but you shall love your neighbor (acquaintance, associate, companion) as yourself; I am the Lord.

AMOS 5:14-16 KING JAMES VERSION (KJV)

¹⁴ Seek good, and not evil, that ye may live: and so the Lord, the God of hosts, shall be with you, as ye have spoken.

¹⁵ Hate the evil, and love the good, and establish judgment in the gate: it may be that the Lord God of hosts will be gracious unto the remnant of Joseph.

¹⁶ Therefore the Lord, the God of hosts, the Lord, saith thus; Wailing shall be in all streets; and they shall say in all the highways, Alas! alas! and they shall call the husbandman to mourning, and such as are skilful of lamentation to wailing.

ROMANS 12:8-10 KING JAMES VERSION (KJV)

⁸ Or he that exhorteth, on exhortation: he that giveth, let him do it with simplicity; he that ruleth, with diligence; he that sheweth mercy, with cheerfulness.

⁹ Let love be without dissimulation. Abhor that which is evil; cleave to that which is good.

¹⁰ Be kindly affectioned one to another with brotherly love; in honour preferring one another;

The provision to love has been engrained in scripture from the times of old. Jesus and His disciples were only expounding upon the teachings of the Old Testament when they taught what is recorded in the New Testament. Remember, God has been teaching His gospel since before time began. In the scripture above we see we are called to love the person and love them enough to rebuke (challenge and point out) their sin and wrong doing. This is shown in scripture by the incident between Jesus and an individual asking about gaining eternal life. The statement that Jesus looked at him and loved him and then told him the error or sin in his life is our example.

> ### MARK 10:17-22 KING JAMES VERSION (KJV)
> [17] *And when he was gone forth into the way, there came one running, and kneeled to him, and asked him, Good Master, what shall I do that I may inherit eternal life?*
> [18] *And Jesus said unto him, Why callest thou me good? there is none good but one, that is, God.*
> [19] *Thou knowest the commandments, Do not commit adultery, Do not kill, Do not steal, Do not bear false witness, Defraud not, Honour thy father and mother.*
> [20] *And he answered and said unto him, Master, all these have I observed from my youth.*
> [21] *Then Jesus beholding him loved him, and said unto him, One thing thou lackest: go thy way, sell whatsoever thou hast, and give to the poor, and thou shalt have treasure in heaven: and come, take up the cross, and follow me.*
> [22] *And he was sad at that saying, and went away grieved: for he had great possessions.*

I am also led to point out, that since Jesus was using the Old Testament as a basis for what He was teaching, for me it also is a conformation that the laws of the Old Testament are still in force. The Old Testament is the foundation of the New Testament and without the Old the New cannot be totally understood. So, we need both to pull together all that God has to offer and teach us. The gospel is like building blocks. Each block depends on the other for strength. We have yet to understand and know all that God wants us to learn. I don't know how many of you realize that there are books mentioned in the Bible that we don't have in our canon of scripture. There are some which others have claimed they have discovered, but we don't know how valid they are except where they agree with what we already have been given. The work of God is ongoing and we will never see an end to His creativeness, nor completely know all there is to know about Him.

ISAIAH 28:9-11 KING JAMES VERSION (KJV)
⁹ Whom shall he teach knowledge? and whom shall he make to understand doctrine? them that are weaned from the milk, and drawn from the breasts.
¹⁰ For precept must be upon precept, precept upon precept; line upon line, line upon line; here a little, and there a little:
¹¹ For with stammering lips and another tongue will he speak to this people.
ISAIAH 28:12-14 KING JAMES VERSION (KJV)
¹² To whom he said, This is the rest wherewith ye may cause the weary to rest; and this is the refreshing: yet they would not hear.
¹³ But the word of the Lord was unto them precept upon precept, precept upon precept; line upon line, line upon line; here a little, and there a little; that they might go, and fall backward, and be broken, and snared, and taken.
¹⁴ Wherefore hear the word of the Lord, ye scornful men, that rule this people which is in Jerusalem.

Science confirms that His creation continues expanding. We can't measure from one end of the Universe to the other nor can we determine the length of time it will take for us to travel from end to end of the portion we do know even at the speed of light. They see the universe is continually expanding. How miniscule we are in comparison.

1 CORINTHIANS 13:8-10 KING JAMES VERSION (KJV)
⁸ Charity never faileth: but whether there be prophecies, they shall fail; whether there be tongues, they shall cease; whether there be knowledge, it shall vanish away.
⁹ For we know in part, and we prophesy in part.
¹⁰ But when that which is perfect is come, then that which is in part shall be done away.

Now let's get back to the teaching of love. God is love, as scripture tells us. We can learn how and what we are to love and how and what we are to hate. The Spirit points us to the references that have to do with God's judgement. First God cannot tolerate sin in the least bit. Yet in His judgement, based on His love for us, He states that He will forgive as long as we repent. Here are two important concepts - forgiveness and repentance. Here we see God first expressing His willingness to love us, yet our acceptance of His love is demonstrated by our willingness to repent. So, love carries with it some requirements on both individuals involved. The first is God's side. The next is our side. God's side cannot be expressed until we accept His offer by showing we will follow His example. You see, repentance is the act of us showing our appreciation for God loving us by us passing this love down to others. It's like God wants us to pass along His love in an unbroken chain to all those we know, hence, following the mandate that Jesus issued in stating "love the Lord your God with all our might mind and strength and love others as neighbor as yourself." Without this there is no gospel or is there any true religion.

1 JOHN 4:18-20 KING JAMES VERSION (KJV)
[18] There is no fear in love; but perfect love casteth out fear: because fear hath torment. He that feareth is not made perfect in love.
[19] We love him, because he first loved us.
[20] If a man say, I love God, and hateth his brother, he is a liar: for he that loveth not his brother whom he hath seen, how can he love God whom he hath not seen?

1 JOHN 4:18-20 AMPLIFIED BIBLE (AMP)
[18] There is no fear in love [dread does not exist]. But perfect (complete, full-grown) love drives out fear, because fear involves [the expectation of divine] punishment, so the one who is afraid [of God's judgment] is not perfected in love [has not grown into a sufficient understanding of God's love].
[19] We love, because [a]He first loved us.
[20] If anyone says, "I love God," and hates (works against) his [Christian] brother he is a liar; for the one who does not love his brother whom he has seen, cannot love God whom he has not seen.

FOOTNOTES:
1 John 4:19 Because God bestowed on humanity a free will, man is not forced to love Him, but rather consciously and freely chooses the response he makes to God's love.

JOHN 14:20-22 KING JAMES VERSION (KJV)
[20] At that day ye shall know that I am in my Father, and ye in me, and I in you.
[21] He that hath my commandments, and keepeth them, he it is that loveth me: and he that loveth me shall be loved of my Father, and I will love him, and will manifest myself to him.
[22] Judas saith unto him, not Iscariot, Lord, how is it that thou wilt manifest thyself unto us, and not unto the world?

JOHN 15:11-13 KING JAMES VERSION (KJV)
[11] These things have I spoken unto you, that my joy might remain in you, and that your joy might be full.

¹² This is my commandment, That ye love one another, as I have loved you.
¹³ Greater love hath no man than this, that a man lay down his life for his friends.

Now let's examine the hate aspect as God presents it in His treatment for those who do not repent or to those who refuse to accept His love and pass it on. Let's review some scripture here.

LEVITICUS 26:42-44 KING JAMES VERSION (KJV)
⁴² Then will I remember my covenant with Jacob, and also my covenant with Isaac, and also my covenant with Abraham will I remember; and I will remember the land.
⁴³ The land also shall be left of them, and shall enjoy her sabbaths, while she lieth desolate without them: and they shall accept of the punishment of their iniquity: because, even because they despised my judgments, and because their soul abhorred my statutes.
⁴⁴ And yet for all that, when they be in the land of their enemies, I will not cast them away, neither will I abhor them, to destroy them utterly, and to break my covenant with them: for I am the Lord their God.

DEUTERONOMY 11:1-3 KING JAMES VERSION (KJV)
¹ Therefore thou shalt love the Lord thy God, and keep his charge, and his statutes, and his judgments, and his commandments, alway.
² And know ye this day: for I speak not with your children which have not known, and which have not seen the chastisement of the Lord your God, his greatness, his mighty hand, and his stretched out arm,
³ And his miracles, and his acts, which he did in the midst of Egypt unto Pharaoh the king of Egypt, and unto all his land;

PSALM 1:4-6 KING JAMES VERSION (KJV)
⁴ The ungodly are not so: but are like the chaff which the wind driveth away.
⁵ Therefore the ungodly shall not stand in the judgment, nor sinners in the congregation of the righteous.
⁶ For the Lord knoweth the way of the righteous: but the way of the ungodly shall perish.

PSALM 9:15-17 KING JAMES VERSION (KJV)
¹⁵ The heathen are sunk down in the pit that they made: in the net which they hid is their own foot taken.
¹⁶ The Lord is known by the judgment which he executeth: the wicked is snared in the work of his own hands. Higgaion. Selah.

[17] *The wicked shall be turned into hell, and all the nations that forget God.*

JUDE 5-7 KING JAMES VERSION (KJV)

[5] *I will therefore put you in remembrance, though ye once knew this, how that the Lord, having saved the people out of the land of Egypt, afterward destroyed them that believed not.*

[6] *And the angels which kept not their first estate, but left their own habitation, he hath reserved in everlasting chains under darkness unto the judgment of the great day.*

[7] *Even as Sodom and Gomorrha, and the cities about them in like manner, giving themselves over to fornication, and going after strange flesh, are set forth for an example, suffering the vengeance of eternal fire.*

Even though we have sinned in our life span, God will forgive those who accept the offer of His love. Those who don't, become part of the sin which He hates. So, when we refuse to repent, we are walking in the role which He is unable to tolerate, we are linked hand in hand with what He hates and that is sin. So as long as a person is walking in sin, he or she is the embodiment of sin and although love is willing and able to accept them when they repent, their hate for God is a refusal of His love and an acceptance to walk in eternal sin. This is why scripture warns against committing the sin against the Holy Ghost. Which is the final plea for us to accept God's invitation for us to accept His call to repentance.

Conclusion

Can love and hate exist in the same sphere? Yes, but not in the way we see hate in the fleshly realm, but the way God wants us to see it in the Godly realm. As stated, before the attributes of love are called out in scripture, stating that love is kind and love is patient... well, I am led share it again here.

GALATIANS 5:21-23 KING JAMES VERSION (KJV)

[21] *Envyings, murders, drunkenness, revellings, and such like: of the which I tell you before, as I have also told you in time past, that they which do such things shall not inherit the kingdom of God.*

[22] *But the fruit of the Spirit is love, joy, peace, longsuffering, gentleness, goodness, faith,*

[23] *Meekness, temperance: against such there is no law.*

LUKE 6:34-36 KING JAMES VERSION (KJV)

34 And if ye lend to them of whom ye hope to receive, what thank have ye? for sinners also lend to sinners, to receive as much again.

35 But love ye your enemies, and do good, and lend, hoping for nothing again; and your reward shall be great, and ye shall be the children of the Highest: for he is kind unto the unthankful and to the evil.

36 Be ye therefore merciful, as your Father also is merciful.

1 CORINTHIANS 13:3-13 KING JAMES VERSION (KJV)

3 And though I bestow all my goods to feed the poor, and though I give my body to be burned, and have not charity, it profiteth me nothing.

4 Charity suffereth long, and is kind; charity envieth not; charity vaunteth not itself, is not puffed up,

5 Doth not behave itself unseemly, seeketh not her own, is not easily provoked, thinketh no evil;

6 Rejoiceth not in iniquity, but rejoiceth in the truth;

7 Beareth all things, believeth all things, hopeth all things, endureth all things.

8 Charity never faileth: but whether there be prophecies, they shall fail; whether there be tongues, they shall cease; whether there be knowledge, it shall vanish away.

9 For we know in part, and we prophesy in part.

10 But when that which is perfect is come, then that which is in part shall be done away.

11 When I was a child, I spake as a child, I understood as a child, I thought as a child: but when I became a man, I put away childish things.

12 For now we see through a glass, darkly; but then face to face: now I know in part; but then shall I know even as also I am known.

13 And now abideth faith, hope, charity, these three; but the greatest of these is charity.

1 CORINTHIANS 13:3-13 AMPLIFIED BIBLE (AMP)

3 If I give all my possessions to feed the poor, and if I surrender my body [a]to be burned, but do not have love, it does me no good at all.

4 Love endures with patience and serenity, love is kind and thoughtful, and is not jealous or envious; love does not brag and is not proud or arrogant. 5 It is not rude; it is not self-seeking, it is not provoked [nor overly sensitive and easily angered]; it does not take into account a wrong endured.

107

6 It does not rejoice at injustice, but rejoices with the truth [when right and truth prevail].

7 Love bears all things [regardless of what comes], believes all things [looking for the best in each one], hopes all things [remaining steadfast during difficult times], endures all things [without weakening].

8 Love never fails [it never fades nor ends]. But as for prophecies, they will pass away; as for tongues, they will cease; as for the gift of special knowledge, it will pass away.

9 For we know in part, and we prophesy in part [for our knowledge is fragmentary and incomplete].

10 But when that which is complete and perfect comes, that which is incomplete and partial will pass away.

11 When I was a child, I talked like a child, I thought like a child, I reasoned like a child; when I became a man, I did away with childish things.

12 For now [in this time of imperfection] we see in a mirror dimly [a blurred reflection, a riddle, an enigma], but then [when the time of perfection comes we will see reality] face to face. Now I know in part [just in fragments], but then I will know fully, just as I have been fully known [by God].

13 And now there remain: faith [abiding trust in God and His promises], hope [confident expectation of eternal salvation], love [unselfish love for others growing out of God's love for me], these three [the choicest graces]; but the greatest of these is love.

FOOTNOTES:

1 Corinthians 13:3 Early mss read so that I may boast, i.e. as a martyr.

Note the word charity in many of the modern translations of the bible is interpreted as Love. God's Love gives not for what it can gain, but for what others may gain. Love is not about what I can get in return, but about doing the good works for the end result it provides. Its power lies in the fact it exists and that no matter what others are or what they choose to be, we are the image of God, selfless and not self-seeking but seeking, the good we can do for others. Though I gain the whole world and have not love I am as a noisy gong or clanging cymbal. I am making a lot of noise which in time fades away and which for a short time draws attention to me and not to God.

CHAPTER 10

Commandments Separate Light From Darkness

JOHN 3:19-21 AMPLIFIED BIBLE (AMP)
19 This is the judgment [that is, the cause for indictment, the test by which people are judged, the basis for the sentence]: the Light has come into the world, and people loved the [a]darkness rather than the Light, for their deeds were evil.
20 For every wrongdoer hates the Light, and does not come to the Light [but shrinks from it] for fear that his [sinful, worthless] activities will be exposed and condemned.
21 But whoever practices truth [and does what is right—morally, ethically, spiritually] comes to the Light, so that his works may be plainly shown to be what they are—accomplished in God [divinely prompted, done with God's help, in dependence on Him]."
FOOTNOTES:
John 3:19 See note 1:5.
1 CORINTHIANS 13:11-13 KING JAMES VERSION (KJV)
11 When I was a child, I spake as a child, I understood as a child, I thought as a child: but when I became a man, I put away childish things.
12 For now we see through a glass, darkly; but then face to face: now I know in part; but then shall I know even as also I am known.
13 And now abideth faith, hope, charity, these three; but the greatest of these is charity.

Darkness in scripture is used to represent the act of living a life other than as God intended while light is used as an analogy of walking in God's principles as He intended. With our eyes in the light we see the full color of the world around us. In the darkness, colors are difficult to impossible to distinguish. Things appear as shades of grey in darkness. Light exposes details while in the dark, the details can be hidden. We see more clearly in the light, while in darkness, shadows make things difficult to see. It is easier to hide things in the darkness than in the light because our vision is diminished. God made it this way for His purpose of showing us the difference between good and evil. Evil is of full of shadowy and even hidden details. God's purpose for night and day is to show that even in His creation, His presence and intelligence can be found. Science has attributed night and day as a phenomenon only due to the earth's rotation. In the cycle of light and darkness we can see there is a great advantage to being in the light. Darkness is the absence of light or the state of diminished light. If you have ever been in one of the huge underground caves you can experience absolute darkness and you gain a real understanding of what true darkness is. When we live our lives in the absence of God's principles it is stated we are walking in darkness.

We as the children of God need to grow up and start on a new path of maturity in Christ. Many today don't see the difference in light and darkness. Scripture tells us that Jesus was the light of the world and that we are to emulate Him. The world has convinced so many that we need to use our reasoning to live our lives and it is not practical to live as Jesus lived because we not perfect as He is. So, we are taught that we should accept the way we are and continue to hold on to the patterns which the world has set. Scripture teaches this not so. Let's see this in scripture.

LUKE 16:7-9 AMPLIFIED BIBLE (AMP)
7 Then he said to another, 'And how much do you owe?' He said, 'A hundred [a]measures of wheat.' He said to him, 'Take your bill, and write eighty.'
8 And his master commended the unjust manager [not for his misdeeds, but] because he had acted shrewdly [by preparing for his future unemployment]; for the sons of this age [the non-believers] are shrewder in relation to their own kind [that is, to the ways of the secular world] than are the sons of light [the believers].

⁹ And I tell you [learn from this], make friends for yourselves [for eternity] by means of the [b]wealth of unrighteousness [that is, use material resources as a way to further the work of God], so that when it runs out, they will welcome you into the eternal dwellings.
FOOTNOTES:
Luke 16:7 Gr kors, one kor equals 10-12 bushels.
Luke 16:9 Gr mamona, from Aram mammon, signifying riches, wealth, etc., personified as an object of worship.
JOHN 12:45-47 KING JAMES VERSION (KJV)
⁴⁵ And he that seeth me seeth him that sent me.
⁴⁶ I am come a light into the world, that whosoever believeth on me should not abide in darkness.
⁴⁷ And if any man hear my words, and believe not, I judge him not: for I came not to judge the world, but to save the world.
JOHN 12:45-47 AMPLIFIED BIBLE (AMP)
⁴⁵ And whoever sees Me sees the One who sent Me.
⁴⁶ I have come as Light into the world, so that everyone who believes and trusts in Me [as Savior—all those who anchor their hope in Me and rely on the truth of My message] will not continue to live in darkness.
⁴⁷ If anyone hears My words and does not keep them, I do not judge him; for I did not come to judge and condemn the world [that is, to initiate the final judgment of the world], but to save the world.
EPHESIANS 2:1-3 AMPLIFIED BIBLE (AMP)
Made Alive in Christ
¹ And you [He made alive when you] were [spiritually] dead and separated from Him because of your transgressions and sins,
² in which you once walked. You were following the ways of this world [influenced by this present age], in accordance with the prince of the power of the air (Satan), the spirit who is now at work in the disobedient [the unbelieving, who fight against the purposes of God].
³ Among these [unbelievers] we all once lived in the passions of our flesh [our behavior governed by the sinful self], indulging the desires of [a]human nature [without the Holy Spirit] and [the impulses] of the [sinful] mind. We were, by nature, children [under the sentence] of [God's] wrath, just like the rest [of mankind].
FOOTNOTES:
Ephesians 2:3 Lit flesh.

Our culture has a lot to do with the way we pattern our lives. We unconsciously accept the norm of our life style and we are often blinded to the traps imbedded in doing this. One such reason for this is that after we accept Christ as our Saviour most do not take the next step because they have not been taught to do this. This step as stated in Scripture is to first seek the Kingdom of God and His righteousness and all these things will be added on to you. Here is some scripture to backup what I am led to tell you.

JOHN 8:4-13 KING JAMES VERSION (KJV)

4 They say unto him, Master, this woman was taken in adultery, in the very act.

5 Now Moses in the law commanded us, that such should be stoned: but what sayest thou?

6 This they said, tempting him, that they might have to accuse him. But Jesus stooped down, and with his finger wrote on the ground, as though he heard them not.

7 So when they continued asking him, he lifted up himself, and said unto them, He that is without sin among you, let him first cast a stone at her.

8 And again he stooped down, and wrote on the ground.

9 And they which heard it, being convicted by their own conscience, went out one by one, beginning at the eldest, even unto the last: and Jesus was left alone, and the woman standing in the midst.

10 When Jesus had lifted up himself, and saw none but the woman, he said unto her, Woman, where are those thine accusers? hath no man condemned thee?

11 She said, No man, Lord. And Jesus said unto her, Neither do I condemn thee: go, and sin no more.

12 Then spake Jesus again unto them, saying, I am the light of the world: he that followeth me shall not walk in darkness, but shall have the light of life.

13 The Pharisees therefore said unto him, Thou bearest record of thyself; thy record is not true.

MATTHEW 5:13-15 KING JAMES VERSION (KJV)

13 Ye are the salt of the earth: but if the salt have lost his savour, wherewith shall it be salted? it is thenceforth good for nothing, but to be cast out, and to be trodden under foot of men.

14 Ye are the light of the world. A city that is set on an hill cannot be hid.

15 Neither do men light a candle, and put it under a bushel, but on a candlestick; and it giveth light unto all that are in the house.

LUKE 16:7-9 KING JAMES VERSION (KJV)
⁷ Then said he to another, And how much owest thou? And he said, An hundred measures of wheat. And he said unto him, Take thy bill, and write fourscore.
⁸ And the lord commended the unjust steward, because he had done wisely: for the children of this world are in their generation wiser than the children of light.
⁹ And I say unto you, Make to yourselves friends of the mammon of unrighteousness; that, when ye fail, they may receive you into everlasting habitations.
2 CORINTHIANS 4:3-5 KING JAMES VERSION (KJV)
³ But if our gospel be hid, it is hid to them that are lost:
⁴ In whom the god of this world hath blinded the minds of them which believe not, lest the light of the glorious gospel of Christ, who is the image of God, should shine unto them.
⁵ For we preach not ourselves, but Christ Jesus the Lord; and ourselves your servants for Jesus' sake.
MATTHEW 6:32-34 KING JAMES VERSION (KJV)
³² (For after all these things do the Gentiles seek:) for your heavenly Father knoweth that ye have need of all these things.
³³ But seek ye first the kingdom of God, and his righteousness; and all these things shall be added unto you.
³⁴ Take therefore no thought for the morrow: for the morrow shall take thought for the things of itself. Sufficient unto the day is the evil thereof.

Let's look into some problems brought about by cultural blindness. I was privileged to be born as a black man. In the United States I have been subjected to living a life where a man or woman is mistreated because of their skin color. I have been called names, not allowed to eat in a restaurant, paid at a lower rate than others who held the same position, not allowed to buy a home in a neighborhood (even though I could afford it) and even graded lower in school. All this because many believe they are superior because they are white. I can go on but hopefully you get the gist of what I am pointing out. Many times, I have pointed these issues out to my white friends, yet they don't see them as problems. Why? First of all, most of them have not had to face all these same issues. Even those whites who are considered at the bottom of the social rung, labeled as "poor white trash," did not have all these types of issues to overcome. Many also have suffered the effects of being culturally blinded by their skin color. Even the so-called poor whites were able to eat at places I could not and go places and buy a house I could not. Sadly, as a result of their skin color, they have privileges (or benefits) which they see as normal and don't see them as anything unusual because they are accustomed to receiving the benefits it provides. Yes, many have been culturally blinded by their skin color. So, when I tell one of my friends, he or she is looking at something from the perspective of a white person, I am pointing out to them that those privileges which they take for granted are not available to me at the present or were not available in the past. Even today in religion the separation continues. We still have white churches and black churches. If you can't see this, look at where most people attend church. Is it not in the neighborhood in which they reside? Aren't most cities in the US segregated into white, black neighborhoods or Jewish, Italian, Hispanic or so on and so forth? Cultural blindness is just as prevalent in the church as it is in the rest of the world. Is this not also true in the educational community in our country where schools in the white neighborhoods are better and higher quality than those in the black neighborhoods?

I should mention that there are many who have chosen, by the love of God that resides in them, to transcend beyond this, just as those who marched hand in hand with the freedom riders and others who have stood for human rights all over the world. There are many who have stood for God and died as a result. The prophets of old and so many others all gave their lives when they stood for the truth in Christ Jesus.

The gospel has been produced to enlighten the church (the people of God) to injustices which exist in the world so they can correct them. Yet many are blind to these because they lack the sensitivity to the issues which others face due to their cultural and social blindness. Here is a case where the conscience of many has been conditioned to accept bias. Scripture tells us to stand for the fatherless and the widows and orphans of this world and that in Christ there is no nationality or racial or sexual bias. Yet many will stand and say, "It's not my fault they suffer these things. It is because of the choices they have made they suffer and are in the situation they are in." Or we take the defense that Cain took and ask the question "Am I my brother's keeper?" The response today is they need 'to get a job' or 'stop being so lazy' or 'they are ignorant' so they deserve their plight. Is that why we do not stop for the beggar on the side of the road?

How about the way the super-rich flaunt their wealth by excluding you without the big bucks from certain privileges? They get to eat in places you can't go. They have special resorts just for them. They have many privileges which only money provides exclusively for them.

Do we not often use the excuse I am a good Christian because I go to church and I follow all the commandments? Is this not the same argument put forth by the person with a lot of wealth who came to Jesus asking what must he do to gain eternal life? Read and meditate on the following scripture.

MATTHEW 19:15-26 KING JAMES VERSION (KJV)

15 And he laid his hands on them, and departed thence.

16 And, behold, one came and said unto him, Good Master, what good thing shall I do, that I may have eternal life?

17 And he said unto him, Why callest thou me good? there is none good but one, that is, God: but if thou wilt enter into life, keep the commandments.

18 He saith unto him, Which? Jesus said, Thou shalt do no murder, Thou shalt not commit adultery, Thou shalt not steal, Thou shalt not bear false witness,

19 Honour thy father and thy mother: and, Thou shalt love thy neighbour as thyself.

20 The young man saith unto him, All these things have I kept from my youth up: what lack I yet?

21 Jesus said unto him, If thou wilt be perfect, go and sell that thou hast, and give to the poor, and thou shalt have treasure in heaven: and come and follow me.

22 But when the young man heard that saying, he went away sorrowful: for he had great possessions.

23 Then said Jesus unto his disciples, Verily I say unto you, That a rich man shall hardly enter into the kingdom of heaven.

24 And again I say unto you, It is easier for a camel to go through the eye of a needle, than for a rich man to enter into the kingdom of God.

25 When his disciples heard it, they were exceedingly amazed, saying, Who then can be saved?

26 But Jesus beheld them, and said unto them, With men this is impossible; but with God all things are possible.

> **MARK 10:15-22 KING JAMES VERSION (KJV)**
> ¹⁵ *Verily I say unto you, Whosoever shall not receive the kingdom of God as a little child, he shall not enter therein.*
> ¹⁶ *And he took them up in his arms, put his hands upon them, and blessed them.*
> ¹⁷ *And when he was gone forth into the way, there came one running, and kneeled to him, and asked him, Good Master, what shall I do that I may inherit eternal life?*
> ¹⁸ *And Jesus said unto him, Why callest thou me good? there is none good but one, that is, God.*
> ¹⁹ *Thou knowest the commandments, Do not commit adultery, Do not kill, Do not steal, Do not bear false witness, Defraud not, Honour thy father and mother.*
> ²⁰ *And he answered and said unto him, Master, all these have I observed from my youth.*
> ²¹ *Then Jesus beholding him loved him, and said unto him, One thing thou lackest: go thy way, sell whatsoever thou hast, and give to the poor, and thou shalt have treasure in heaven: and come, take up the cross, and follow me.*
> ²² *And he was sad at that saying, and went away grieved: for he had great possessions.*

Conclusion

We are called to move beyond the gospel of repentance from dead works and move forward into doing and performing those things which bring forth the light of the living gospel, creating the same conditions on earth as they are in heaven. The gospel is not a shorted-sited, self-centered approach which just involves us and our personal walk but taking up our cross dying to sin and walking in a new way which produces good works. You see the part of the gospel which has to do with repentance from dead works should free us to do good works, but the church seems to be stuck just as the same as the person in the scripture below requesting what he should do to gain eternal life.

> **LUKE 10:25-37 KING JAMES VERSION (KJV)**
> ²⁵ *And, behold, a certain lawyer stood up, and tempted him, saying, Master, what shall I do to inherit eternal life?*
> ²⁶ *He said unto him, What is written in the law? how readest thou?*

^{27} And he answering said, Thou shalt love the Lord thy God with all thy heart, and with all thy soul, and with all thy strength, and with all thy mind; and thy neighbour as thyself.

^{28} And he said unto him, Thou hast answered right: this do, and thou shalt live.

^{29} But he, willing to justify himself, said unto Jesus, And who is my neighbour?

^{30} And Jesus answering said, A certain man went down from Jerusalem to Jericho, and fell among thieves, which stripped him of his raiment, and wounded him, and departed, leaving him half dead.

^{31} And by chance there came down a certain priest that way: and when he saw him, he passed by on the other side.

^{32} And likewise a Levite, when he was at the place, came and looked on him, and passed by on the other side.

^{33} But a certain Samaritan, as he journeyed, came where he was: and when he saw him, he had compassion on him,

^{34} And went to him, and bound up his wounds, pouring in oil and wine, and set him on his own beast, and brought him to an inn, and took care of him.

^{35} And on the morrow when he departed, he took out two pence, and gave them to the host, and said unto him, Take care of him; and whatsoever thou spendest more, when I come again, I will repay thee.

^{36} Which now of these three, thinkest thou, was neighbour unto him that fell among the thieves?

^{37} And he said, He that shewed mercy on him. Then said Jesus unto him, Go, and do thou likewise.

Note in this account from Luke we see that Jesus substitutes a parable for His expression "take up your cross," which was previously quoted. Taking up one's cross was a real mystery to all who heard it then and even to this day. Here, Jesus uses a parable to bring further enlightenment to those who are willing to receive it. Many misunderstand parables to be a way Jesus brought further explanation to those He was talking to, but this is not the case. He spoke in parables to confuse those who were not serious about following His teachings. In the following scripture He states this.

PSALM 78:1-11 KING JAMES VERSION (KJV)

^{1} Give ear, O my people, to my law: incline your ears to the words of my mouth.

^{2} I will open my mouth in a parable: I will utter dark sayings of old:

³ Which we have heard and known, and our fathers have told us.
⁴ We will not hide them from their children, shewing to the generation to come the praises of the Lord, and his strength, and his wonderful works that he hath done.
⁵ For he established a testimony in Jacob, and appointed a law in Israel, which he commanded our fathers, that they should make them known to their children:
⁶ That the generation to come might know them, even the children which should be born; who should arise and declare them to their children:
⁷ That they might set their hope in God, and not forget the works of God, but keep his commandments:
⁸ And might not be as their fathers, a stubborn and rebellious generation; a generation that set not their heart aright, and whose spirit was not stedfast with God.
MATTHEW 13:9-11 KING JAMES VERSION (KJV)
⁹ Who hath ears to hear, let him hear.
¹⁰ And the disciples came, and said unto him, Why speakest thou unto them in parables?
¹¹ He answered and said unto them, Because it is given unto you to know the mysteries of the kingdom of heaven, but to them it is not given.
MATTHEW 16:23-25 KING JAMES VERSION (KJV)
²³ But he turned, and said unto Peter, Get thee behind me, Satan: thou art an offence unto me: for thou savourest not the things that be of God, but those that be of men.
²⁴ Then said Jesus unto his disciples, If any man will come after me, let him deny himself, and take up his cross, and follow me.
²⁵ For whosoever will save his life shall lose it: and whosoever will lose his life for my sake shall find it.

Jesus used parables to provide an explanation for those who genuinely wanted to know His purposes, those who were searching with the true intent of understanding the meaning of God's plan for man. To all others, they are just a short story line or a riddle. Those who really want to understand will study them with prayer and seek, by the power of the Holy Spirit, God's true intent and purpose behind them.

The parable, in Luke 10 above, just as the statement "take up my cross" in Matthew 19 above, is still a mystery to most of the church. They continue to promote it as a directive to follow the Ten Commandments rather than moving into a more perfect state as Jesus points to. Why is it we walk so blindly to the ultimate purpose of God's intent which is to prove good will overcome evil?

I will close by repeating something I was led to include earlier. In Psalms 8, I pointed out that God in the end will show that we were created to prove God's goodness will overcome the evil or His light will expose all evil and light will prevail. Here it is again.

PSALM 8:1-9 KING JAMES VERSION (KJV)

1 O Lord, our Lord, how excellent is thy name in all the earth! who hast set thy glory above the heavens.

2 Out of the mouth of babes and sucklings hast thou ordained strength because of thine enemies, that thou mightest still the enemy and the avenger.

3 When I consider thy heavens, the work of thy fingers, the moon and the stars, which thou hast ordained;

4 What is man, that thou art mindful of him? and the son of man, that thou visitest him?

5 For thou hast made him a little lower than the angels, and hast crowned him with glory and honour.

6 Thou madest him to have dominion over the works of thy hands; thou hast put all things under his feet:

7 All sheep and oxen, yea, and the beasts of the field;

8 The fowl of the air, and the fish of the sea, and whatsoever passeth through the paths of the seas.

9 O Lord our Lord, how excellent is thy name in all the earth!

HEBREWS 2:1-13 KING JAMES VERSION (KJV)

1 Therefore we ought to give the more earnest heed to the things which we have heard, lest at any time we should let them slip.

2 For if the word spoken by angels was stedfast, and every transgression and disobedience received a just recompence of reward;

3 How shall we escape, if we neglect so great salvation; which at the first began to be spoken by the Lord, and was confirmed unto us by them that heard him;

4 God also bearing them witness, both with signs and wonders, and with divers miracles, and gifts of the Holy Ghost, according to his own will?

5 For unto the angels hath he not put in subjection the world to come, whereof we speak.

6 But one in a certain place testified, saying, What is man, that thou art mindful of him? or the son of man that thou visitest him?

⁷ Thou madest him a little lower than the angels; thou crownedst him with glory and honour, and didst set him over the works of thy hands:

⁸ Thou hast put all things in subjection under his feet. For in that he put all in subjection under him, he left nothing that is not put under him. But now we see not yet all things put under him.

⁹ But we see Jesus, who was made a little lower than the angels for the suffering of death, crowned with glory and honour; that he by the grace of God should taste death for every man.

¹⁰ For it became him, for whom are all things, and by whom are all things, in bringing many sons unto glory, to make the captain of their salvation perfect through sufferings.

¹¹ For both he that sanctifieth and they who are sanctified are all of one: for which cause he is not ashamed to call them brethren,

¹² Saying, I will declare thy name unto my brethren, in the midst of the church will I sing praise unto thee.

¹³ And again, I will put my trust in him. And again, Behold I and the children which God hath given me.

In Psalm 8 and also Hebrews 2 we have a glimpse of how highly God regards man. Wow! Is it not a privilege to be set on such a high pedestal? Not only does it state God's purpose in creating us it also provides insight into His ultimate will for us. Note verse 2 in Psalm 8 where it is stated that He intends to silence the enemy and the avenger. Do you understand this statement? Do you know who the enemy of God is and who is the avenger?

Finally, Jesus statements:

JOHN 8:11-13 KING JAMES VERSION (KJV)

¹⁰ When Jesus had lifted up himself, and saw none but the woman, he said unto her, Woman, where are those thine accusers? hath no man condemned thee?

¹¹ She said, No man, Lord. And Jesus said unto her, Neither do I condemn thee: go, and sin no more.

¹² Then spake Jesus again unto them, saying, I am the light of the world: he that followeth me shall not walk in darkness, but shall have the light of life.

¹³ The Pharisees therefore said unto him, Thou bearest record of thyself; thy record is not true.

JOHN 8:10-13 AMPLIFIED BIBLE (AMP)

¹⁰ Straightening up, Jesus said to her, "Woman, where are they? Did no one condemn you?"

[11] She answered, "No one, Lord!" And Jesus said, "I do not condemn you either. Go. From now on sin no more."]

Jesus Is the Light of the World

[12] Once more Jesus addressed the crowd. He said, "[a]I am the Light of the world. He who follows Me will not walk in the darkness, but will have the Light of life."

[13] Then the Pharisees told Him, "You are testifying on Your own behalf; Your testimony is not valid."

FOOTNOTES:

John 8:12 The second of the memorable "I am" statements. See note 6:35.

JOHN 9:4-6 KING JAMES VERSION (KJV)

[4] I must work the works of him that sent me, while it is day: the night cometh, when no man can work.

[5] As long as I am in the world, I am the light of the world

[6] When he had thus spoken, he spat on the ground, and made clay of the spittle, and he anointed the eyes of the blind man with the clay,

JOHN 11:8-10 KING JAMES VERSION (KJV)

[8] His disciples say unto him, Master, the Jews of late sought to stone thee; and goest thou thither again?

[9] Jesus answered, Are there not twelve hours in the day? If any man walk in the day, he stumbleth not, because he seeth the light of this world.

[10] But if a man walk in the night, he stumbleth, because there is no light in him.

[6] When he had thus spoken, he spat on the ground, and made clay of the spittle, and he anointed the eyes of the blind man with the clay,

Is there a more fitting quote to end on than with what Jesus ended His teaching on the sermon on the mount with the statement provided in Matthew 5?

MATTHEW 5:43-48 KING JAMES VERSION (KJV)

43 Ye have heard that it hath been said, Thou shalt love thy neighbour, and hate thine enemy.

44 But I say unto you, Love your enemies, bless them that curse you, do good to them that hate you, and pray for them which despitefully use you, and persecute you;

45 That ye may be the children of your Father which is in heaven: for he maketh his sun to rise on the evil and on the good, and sendeth rain on the just and on the unjust.

46 For if ye love them which love you, what reward have ye? do not even the publicans the same?

47 And if ye salute your brethren only, what do ye more than others? do not even the publicans so?

48 Be ye therefore perfect, even as your Father which is in heaven is perfect.

Appendix

Scripture References

About the Author

OR SCRIBE (AS I SEE IT)

Lorenzo Hill and his wife Clotilde right after marriage, 1969

Lorenzo Hill and his wife Clotilde after 49 years, 2018

Lorenzo Hill has served in the ministry of the Community of Christ (formerly The Reorganized Church of Jesus Christ Of Latter Day Saints) since 1976, when he was ordained a priest. Throughout his ministry, he has been a self-supporting minister. He has served in his current office of Evangelist since 1988 and continues to be very active in ministry, serving in various roles of leadership and other roles in which he is called to serve. His passion has been providing guidance to youth. He had to sadly stop this part of his ministry for health reasons. He provides ongoing ministry through his commitment to spreading word in preaching and bringing ministry to the sick in soul and body.

Lorenzo was raised in St. Louis Missouri and resided there until he received his Bachelor of Science degree in Chemical Engineering in 1970 from the University of Missouri at Rolla (currently known as the Missouri School of Science and Technology). He is a registered retired professional engineer. He has worked in the petroleum industry since he graduated from college and has retired twice. Needless to say, he has moved around quite a bit. He has been blessed to be able to see many other countries because of his employment and for pleasure. The Holy Spirit has used this to open his eyes to the suffering that many experience in this life due to governmental policies and personal lifestyles.

He has been married to his wife, Clotilde for 49 years. She has been his constant support in all his endeavors. They have three children: Alicia Renee Hill, Reynada Charlese Robinson, and one son, Jared Lorenzo Hill.

Although he has taken many post graduate courses in both engineering and ministry, Lorenzo chose not to pursue an advanced degree. He has written numerous technical reports and technical texts for the training and instruction of engineers and construction inspectors. All of these works, however, were prepared for either clients or for internal company use and as such, were not issued as external publications.

He was inspired to publish one book prior to this endeavor. This book is titled:
Formulas In The Scripture
E =MC2
THE KEY TO OUR PENTECOST EXPERIENCE.

This work is currently in print and can be purchased on Amazon.com in paperback or e-book format.
He has been inspired to start working on a third book at this time which is to be titled:
Eternal Life
Going beyond the Basics of Repentance, Solid food.
This work is projected to be in print by the end of 2019 or early 2020.

If there is one way to express His walk with Christ there are some words from a hymn in our church entitled admonition. These are as follows:
Grace waits upon the souls who try.
Thanks to my wife and daughters for assisting in these works. Praise be to God for His guidance and encouragement.

Made in the USA
Columbia, SC
04 May 2019